Forty Years
AT SAQUISH BEACH
Our Impossible Dream

Forty Years
AT SAQUISH BEACH
Our Impossible Dream

Connie Matuzek

Forty Years At Saquish Beach: *Our Impossible Dream*
©2024 by Connie Matuzek All rights reserved.

No part of this book may be reproduced or transmitted in any form or by any means, electronic or mechanical, including photocopying, recording, or by any information storage and retrieval system, without permission in writing from the copyright owner.

Published by **Connie Matuzek**

ISBN: 979-8-89021-319-8 Paperback
ISBN: 979-8-89021-320-4 Hardback
ISBN: 979-8-89021-318-1 eBook

Printed in the United States of America

This book is printed on acid-free paper.

CONTENTS

Acknowledgments xi
Prelude xiii

Chapter 1:   The Beginning 1
Chapter 2:   The Roads Of Saquish & The Peninsula 6
Chapter 3:   The Start Of Construction 10
Chapter 4:   The First Summer 18
Chapter 5:   Finishing Construction 22
Chapter 6:   Growing Up 26
Chapter 7:   The Impossible Dream 39
Chapter 8:   Additions, Enhancements And Renovations 50
Chapter 9:   Shellfish 59
Chapter 10:   Cod, Flounder, & Other Fish 63
Chapter 11:   Lobstering 71
Chapter 12:   Striped Bass And Bluefish 81
Chapter 13:   The Priests From Miramar 92
Chapter 14:   Our Pets, Jake, Sport, Sox And Casey 96
Chapter 15:   Wildlife 103
Chapter 16:   Nature 110
Chapter 17"   The Gurnet - Saquish Association 117
Chapter 18:   Remembrances 124

About The Author 143

FOR MY FAMILY ANN
KATHI AND FRANZ LORRI AND BRIAN
CORY, SYDNEY, MICHAEL and MAX

I LOVE ALL OF YOU

ACKNOWLEDGMENTS

To Ann my partner for the forty years at Saquish and who was the overall coordinator for the activities that brought this book to fruition.

To Sue Judge and Chuck McLaughlin whose professional backgrounds and experience were of great value in the editing process.

To Marv Bell whose knowledge and work with digital photography renewed some old photographs and brought them to life again.

And to all our friends and relatives, who either lived or visited us at Saquish. You helped make our forty years there so enjoyable and memorable.

Thanks to each and everyone of you.

PRELUDE

Before spending a weekend thirty miles southeast of Boston on a remote peninsula we had no idea that we would spend forty years enjoying the ambience and lifestyle of Saquish Beach. Saquish is of American Indian origin meaning "place of many clams."

Even more remote was any idea that someday I would write a Biographical Memoir with eighteen individual and unique chapters. They describe what it was like to spend Spring and Summer living on a remote beach and enjoying all the experiences that it has to offer, similar to living at a cottage on the ocean, a bay, a lake, a river or anywhere else that is off the beaten path.

For years my wife Ann encouraged me to write a story of how we built the cottage. It was built at a place with no public roads or amenities, nor any commercial electric or telephone service. With no electricity, power tools were never used. The story would provide a written history for our two daughters, sons-in-law and four grandchildren, of how we built it and what we experienced.

My story begins by telling how Ann and I met, bought land and transported 30 tons of building material and furnishings over the beaches and sand dunes with a 4-wheel drive SUV and boat trailer, often getting bogged down in the sand. It describes how we excavated, sawed and drilled everything by hand in building the cottage, just like in the days of the pioneers.

Before starting this project, I couldn't bang a nail in straight. If we had to rely on me using my hands to make a living, we would have starved to death. Thankfully my sixty-year-old dad, who was in the construction field, and my mother partnered with us.

Ann also encouraged me to include the process we went through over twenty years later, in acquiring a permit for a second story observation room. Plymouth had ceased issuing permits for any building additions a number of years before, when Saquish was classified as a wetlands area. The issues and complexities of dealing with the permitting process were intensive. After a couple years of frustration, success prevailed and we finally acquired the permit.

The observation room provides a 360° view. It encompasses the open ocean, Plymouth Beach, Clarks Island, the Back Bay, Powder Point Bridge, the access road to and from Duxbury, Gurnet Point and The Gurnet Lighthouse. In the morning and evening you can see the sun and then the moon rise out of the ocean.

Before I started to write, pleasant memories would come to mind. For a few years I would just jot them down and file them. As I talked to friends and told them about writing my story, they would ask if I had included this event or that scenario in which they were involved. This would often trigger a few more memories and they were also noted.

The eighteen chapters are a result of organizing my thoughts and notes in a logical manner. Each one stands on its own, yet there is a feeling of life on a remote beach and surrounding ocean that transcends and unites all of them.

The chapter titled GROWING UP relates the beach experiences, activities and stories of our two daughters, Kathi and Lorri. Watching them mature and then recalling many specifics was enlightening and enjoyable.

A number of the stories include our four grandchildren Cory, Sydney, Michael and Max. These are stories to which all parents and grandparents can relate.

In Duxbury there is a seminary, named Miramar, run by the Divine Word Missionaries. Fifty years ago the Bishop gave them the authority to say Mass at Saquish due to its remoteness. Every Saturday afternoon they say Mass on the beach or on a sand dune in front of a cottage. In the evening they have dinner at someone's cottage. My book covers the activities of the missionaries and their interaction with the people of Saquish.

There are chapters on shellfish (clamming), lobstering and fishing. The fishing chapters feature flounder, cod, striped bass and bluefish. An attempt at tuna fishing is also discussed. These are based on forty years of personal experience coupled with the first hand knowledge I gained.

I describe what we did, including the related when, where, how and why. The resulting fishing successes and problems encountered are highlighted. There are a number of unique stories about specific events that took place while participating in these fishing and lobstering activities.

As in other chapters, a majority of these stories are positive, some are humorous and others are out-and-out funny. On the other side of the equation there are a few instances that were life-threatening.

Nature by its very nature mimics the saying, "The Good, The Bad and The Ugly." A couple of the good include looking at a double rainbow that stretches from the open ocean 180º across to the mainland. Drifting on the gentle swell of an outgoing tide on a calm early morning, and watching the sunrise over the ocean is hard to beat. The thrill of catching a striped bass or two can also make any good day better.

Nature's bad side is lightning hitting a cottage. Or it could be a car on a sand bar flooded by the incoming tide.

The truly ugly occurred twice. They were the Blizzard of '78 and the No Name Storm of '91, AKA "The Perfect Storm." They both caused extensive devastation on our peninsula and the rehabilitation work was substantial.

Our pets have a chapter all to themselves. It covers their uniqueness and idiosyncrasies during their beach adventures. People who enjoy pets will find this interesting.

The chapter on wildlife covers forty years of observing and interacting with the numerous types of animals that inhabited or have passed through the peninsula. This covers the spectrum from seagulls, to Snowy Owls, to a family of coyotes and finally to a beached Pilot Whale. The whale was beached late one evening, and then what happened is very interesting.

I have lightly touched on some of the chapters in my book and hopefully have provided a taste of what's included. Life on Saquish gave us much joy and many pleasant memories, as did the writing of this story. Both endeavors were labors of love.

As you continue to Chapter 1 "THE BEGINNING" and the other chapters, hopefully you will share in the thrill and enjoyment that Ann and I experienced.

CHAPTER 1
THE BEGINNING

Ann and I met on Saturday, October 6, 1962, at Sandy and Gene Wojnar's wedding.

Since Ann was the best-looking young lady there, with the cutest smile and an apparent positive up-beat personality, I asked her to dance. During the dance, we introduced ourselves then danced again. After the second dance was over we stopped and were talking in the middle of the dance floor. I saw my Aunt Helen strolling across the dance floor and headed toward us. I told Ann that since graduating from college, every time Helen saw me she asked me when I was getting married. I asked Ann if it was O.K. to introduce her as my fiancé and asked her again what her last name was.

Ann was a sport and played the role. After we told Helen about our newly established plan, she next asked what day we had chosen for our wedding. I told her we had not yet chosen a date, after all we had just met, but would let her know when we did. After Helen left we laughed about the made up story and at the end of the wedding celebration Ann and I agreed to see a movie together the next evening, our first date. Unbeknown to each other, we both were at the end of existing romances and each of us broke them off that Saturday night. The rest, as they say, is history. We were married on May 2, 1964, a year and a half later.

By then Sandy and Gene had bought land at Saquish Beach and built a cottage. They invited us to join them at their new beach location for a summer weekend.

The trip to Saquish was a challenge. We drove to the St. George Street garage in Duxbury, MA. parked behind the garage, and paid Mr. Prince, the garage owner, $5 to drive us to our destination. He used a 4-wheel drive dump truck, where Ann and I sat in the open cargo area in the back.

We bounced over a wooden bridge and took a cross over through a sand dune onto a barren beach, with no idea where we were or where we were going. A couple of miles down the beach, we crossed back over the sand dune. Directly in front of us was a large marsh. A dirt road went to the left and up on to a large knoll that had a quaint village named, The Gurnet, and a picturesque lighthouse, named Gurnet Light.

We later found out that the lighthouse was built in 1769 and shortly thereafter a fort was constructed near it. During the Revolutionary War, the lighthouse was hit by a wild cannon shot from a British frigate that had gone aground on Brown's Bank. A quaint bit of history.

The truck continued its bouncing ride up and over The Gurnet then down past three cottages, over another sand dune and onto a beautiful white sandy beach called Saquish. We both looked at each other and said, "Wow." We never knew a place like this existed. Saquish is a private beach located on a remote peninsula 25 miles southeast of Boston. The peninsula starts in Marshfield, extends through Duxbury, and then becomes part of Plymouth, even though it is not connected to Plymouth by land. It is accessible from a bridge that crosses the bay from Duxbury to Duxbury Beach.

On the peninsula there were 220 summer homes and cottages but no town roads or services, nor any commercial electricity, natural gas or telephone service. It is very much like a remote island in the Caribbean.

We fell in love with Saquish and considered buying land there. We started to save money, but after Kathi was born on May 11, 1966, I was transferred to New York City and we bought a house in New Jersey. On November 4, 1968, Lorri was born. After four years in New York, we were transferred back to Westboro, MA. where we had a new house built. The profit on the Jersey house was substantial and we decided to buy land at Saquish.

One of my striper fishing friends in N.J. was an executive at International Harvester and for $50 over factory cost he offered to have a 4-wheel drive vehicle delivered to a dealer in MA. He told us to contact him and order the vehicle when we bought the land.

When we arrived in MA. we saw Gene and he called George Cavanaugh, a major land owner at Saquish. George was willing to meet with us and sell us a lot, but the price was four times what it was four years before. After much consternation, we decided to buy, believing that land next to water was only going to increase in value. This, coupled with our belief that there was no better place to raise two young daughters than a summer cottage on a remote ocean beach, made the decision easy.

There were two lots available, located between Goose Gosselin's and Richard Balakier's cottages. Since we knew Goose, we bought the lot next to his. It was financially impossible for us to build for a number of years, so my father who worked in the construction industry and my mother, offered to go into a partnership with us on the purchase of the land and to start building immediately. At that time you could no longer build on beach front lots, so the lot in front of us was not for sale.

As soon as we signed the contract to buy the land, we ordered an International Harvester 4-wheel drive SUV. It was Harvest-Gold and had wood grain paneling. In the dealer's picture it looked beautiful. We were promised delivery in four to six weeks. The four to six weeks turned into four months, and when it arrived the color was bright canary yellow. There was quite a difference when you looked at a small picture and compared it to the large vehicle. Our girls named it the "Yellow Bird." From then on all our friends called it by that name.

At that time, I was carpooling with four of my friends who all worked in Boston I had told them about the beautiful Harvest- Gold SUV that I was getting. The day after the canary looking SUV arrived, it was my day to drive. As I stopped to pickup each friend they individually gave me a puzzled questionable look, but no one said a word until we were half way to Boston. Then the joking started. It all revolved around the bright canary yellow color of my new SUV and the man made rules of the road that many Boston drivers followed.

The first rule was that vehicles and not pedestrians had the right of way, so pedestrians could clearly see me coming and could easily step back on the curb to get out of the way. The second rule was that when entering an intersection where many streets came together and there were no stop signs or traffic lights, of which Boston had many, the vehicle that was the biggest followed by the brightest and then the oldest had the right of way. All the other vehicles were lumped together and fell into fourth place. My friends all agreed that my new SUV was not the biggest and definitely not the oldest, but in brightness it was superseded only by a school bus, so we had moved from fourth to second place. This was the last time my commuter friends made any comments about my canary yellow SUV.

In the early seventies there were few vehicle manufacturers that made an SUV, and International Harvester made the biggest. Over the next few years the "Yellow Bird" proved invaluable in carrying large loads of materials and furnishings on our many trips to the beach.

The Saturday after the Boston trip Ann, Kathi, Lorri, Mom, Dad and I took a trip to Saquish to see the land we had bought. This was the first time my mother and the girls would see it. We didn't know how to handle a four wheel drive and bogged down in the sand a couple of times, but finally made it. Everyone loved Saquish, especially the girls, who fell in love with the beach.

We then bought an 18' Penn Yan boat and trailer. The boat was stored in a barn in Grafton, and we built sideboards for the trailer to use it for hauling building materials. Arrangements were made with a friend of ours, who was a foreman for a line crew at the telephone company, to obtain telephone poles that were knocked down by cars or replaced for other reasons.

If the pole was not in a residential area it could be left there overnight. He would call us each time a good pole was available. This saved his company the time and expense of sawing it into three foot pieces and taking it to the dump.

My grandfather had given us a 5' long two man hand saw that he had at his farm. He cut down large trees with it that were used as fire wood to heat his house. In the evening, after receiving a telephone call, we would pick up the telephone pole using the boat trailer, the saw and a pair of antique ice tongs that Ann bought at a garage sale. From the pole, we would cut out the best 16' piece that was available and with the ice tongs lift it onto the trailer and tie it down. Next we would remove the large 10" galvanized bolts along with the washers and nuts that were attached to the pole and store them for future use. The ice tongs proved helpful through the initial construction project anytime poles were moved and the saw proved very useful in cutting and notching large timbers.

Ann's sister Dot had just married Tom Kelley, a Train Master for the railroad company. He was able to find us brand new double length railroad ties which we used for the center row of our foundation. His company had stored them in a remote location where they were going to build tracks to turn railroad engines around and repair them. When their plans changed, they no longer needed the ties. This was a win-win situation. His company also saved the costs involved in the removal of the ties and we saved the expense of buying twenty-four poles for the foundation. The telephone poles and railroad ties were stored on the right side of our front yard in Westboro.

In the late fall of 1970, with six poles loaded on the trailer, Ann, Kathi, Lorri, my father, mother and I made a second trip to Saquish.

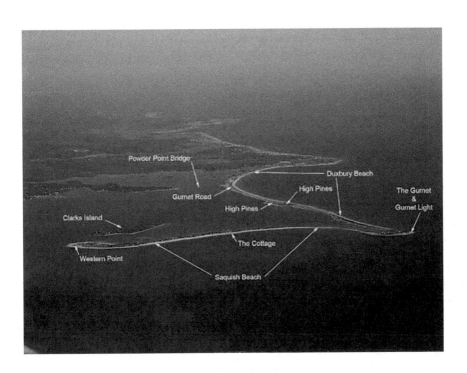

THE PENINSULA

CHAPTER 2

THE ROADS OF SAQUISH & THE PENINSULA

Once you were in Duxbury you drove to the Powder Point Bridge, which was over a half mile long. It is one of the longest wooden bridges in the United States.

You then left the public road, drove over the bridge and arrived at the Duxbury Beach parking lot. From there the distance to our property, which was located right in the middle of Saquish Beach, was five miles. Hopefully, the drive was over a firm hard beach for a good part of the way. To the end of the peninsula, at Western Point, was more than another mile from the cottage.

At that time there were six crossovers between the Duxbury Beach side of the peninsula, which fronted on Cape Cod Bay, and the Duxbury Bay side which nestled on the village of Snug Harbor and the Duxbury Marina. The first crossover was right through the Duxbury Beach parking lot and went through the small sand dune directly on to the beach.

This was the main crossover used to access Saquish. The next two were before High Pines, which was a large area with one cottage, located a couple of miles down the beach. These were used if the tide was too high to cross in front of High Pines. In that case, you had to cross back over the sand dune before High Pines and use the soft sandy road on the bay side.

The fourth was just beyond High Pines and was the major crossover to a combined hard packed rocky dirt and sandy road on the bay side. This was an extension of the soft sandy road that went behind High Pines. Once there you would stay on the bay side until you reached The Gurnet, a small, high elevated village that contained Gurnet Light. This crossover had a moderate incline from the beach to the bay and had a stretch of small round rocks before you reached the top of the incline. If you approached the incline when the ocean was at mid-tide or lower you could gain enough speed to easily reach the road on the back bay.

The fifth crossover was closer to The Gurnet and had a much steeper incline and small rocks that resembled ball bearings. If the tide was low and you had a fast start you made it. If not you might bog down in those ball bearing like rocks and were in for some work.

The sixth and last crossover was right before The Gurnet. This one was treacherous and was used when exiting the beach on a very low tide. When entering from the beach it was very steep, comprised of soft sand and slippery rocks. Quite often the sand below the high tide level was soft and your tires would sink in a few inches and inhibit the speed necessary to make the incline. This crossover, in driving to Saquish, was not for the faint of heart. A bogged down vehicle could become flooded by the incoming tide. This happened every now and then. In short, the use of specific crossovers were determined by tides, sand conditions and the fortitude of the driver.

From two hours after high tide until two hours before it, you would use the crossover at the parking lot and the first one beyond High Pines to drive to and from the Gurnet. Otherwise you used the cart path through the sand dunes from the parking lot to the soft sandy road behind High Pines.

After reaching The Gurnet, you were on high ground driving on a one lane gravel road. From there, traffic exiting the beach had the right of way. You took the first right hand turn and came down to a lowland area. During a very high tide the lowland area would flood, but you could circle around the lowland using the one lane roads on The Gurnet, then come back around to Saquish Beach.

Once at Saquish, except during a high tide, you would ride the front beach. The plot plan for Saquish showed a road between the beach and the first row of lots that was named the Boulevard. The Boulevard was nothing more than part of the sandy beach, which was often covered by the ocean on a moon tide. If the tide was high you could use the Back Road that was between the last row of cottages and the Back Bay. This was a combination of sand and gravel, mostly packed sand. On an extremely high tide, neither was accessible, and you might have to wait up to three or more hours for the tide to recede. Connecting the front beach and the bay are a number of streets, often referred to by other names, such as cart paths. Some of the streets are composed of soft sand and others are totally impassable because of the sand dunes that have drifted, or the vegetation that has grown over them. During the dry hot summer months, the soft sand often becomes very soft sand and many vehicles would get stuck.

At the end of the beach, the Back Road merges with the Boulevard. There were times when the sand had built up and the tides were very low, that it was possible to continue driving on the beach all the way to Western Point which was the end of the peninsula, but this seldom occurred. A short distance after the roads merged there was a right turn that took you into an area that was called The Head and it contained a number of cottages. From here there were two ways to get to Western point and the beach that was there. If the tide was low, you would drive straight ahead to the bay. Then you would travel over a rocky area that turned into a very sandy cart path.

After taking the initial right turn, you could always take an immediate left. This was a right of way known as the "Goat Trail." This trail went past a number of cottages, climbed over the top of The Head and then became a steep incline. It consisted of many large imbedded rocks and once past the cottages, thick shrubbery grew up against it on both sides. Traveling over it was the bumpiest of any ride on the peninsula. If two vehicles met in the middle, one of them would have to back up or back down for a considerable distance. After reaching the bottom of the incline, the trail merged with the sandy cart path and then it was on to the beach at Western Point.

These were the roads, crossovers, cart paths, trail and driving conditions that we dealt with, during our first twenty years at Saquish.

After the No Name Storm of '91, Duxbury made extensive repairs and changes in accessing its beach and The Gurnet-Saquish area. A two lane gravel road was installed close to and parallel with the bay. It went all the way from the parking lot to The Gurnet. All traffic going to The Gurnet or Saquish had to use the two lane gravel road and could no longer crossover and use Duxbury Beach. The first, fourth, fifth and sixth crossovers were closed to residential traffic. The second and third crossovers were used to access the beach by people that had Duxbury Beach permits. The gravel road made traveling from the parking lot to The Gurnet much easier and eliminated all concerns about tide levels.

The Gurnet-Saquish Association has continually maintained the Back Road, trying to improve areas that have deteriorated from storms or heavy usage. Everything else regarding the roads and driving conditions has stayed the same as it was forty years ago. Thankfully improved technology, especially in 4-wheel drive vehicles has made driving in remote areas a little easier.

On that second trip using the trailer to haul six poles, we went directly onto Duxbury Beach and took the third crossover right before High Pines. With little familiarity of the crossovers, this was the wrong one. It had the soft sand trail to get around High Pines. The SUV bogged down a couple of times.

We shoveled out the back and front wheels on the SUV and the two wheels on the trailer, jacked both of them up, put some boards and stones under the wheels, accelerated the SUV and tried to plow through the soft sand to a harder, firmer spot. When we didn't make it far enough, we had to repeat the process as many times as it took. Our two young girls, two and four years old, thought that this was hilarious. Driving over the bumpy wooden bridge, then riding right next to the ocean and finally getting stuck in the sand a few times was the most excitement they had ever had. Their only regret was that their sand shovels and pails were left at home.

This type of experience was encountered by most of the Saquish residents, some occasionally others frequently. We were of the frequent variety as we hauled the thirty tons of building material and furniture over the next number of years. That day we finally made it to Saquish, unloaded the poles in the back of our lot, and then returned home with no further problems.

The next steps were preparing for the initial stages of construction during the Fall and Winter and then starting construction in early March 1971.

CHAPTER 3

THE START OF CONSTRUCTION

During the Fall and Winter of 1970, we continued to collect telephone poles when we received a call that one was available. The two man crosscut saw was used to cut the best 16' long piece from each pole. They were then stored at our home in Westboro on the corner of our front yard with the other poles. The neighbors knew they would disappear by early Spring.

I contacted a number of prefabrication companies and received layouts that they used. The design we chose was a 24' x 40' building with a complete wrap around porch and walkway, 8' in front and back and 3' on each side. This required 24 poles for the foundation.

The interior was a combination of layouts that Ann and I redesigned to maximize living space, closets, a combination kitchen and den, three bedrooms and two bathrooms. The second bathroom had an exit door leading out to the walkway right where a hand pump was placed. This would allow everyone to wash the sand off their feet before entering the cottage. We filed for a building permit with Plymouth and received it within a few weeks.

In the middle of the Winter, a contractor that Dad knew was tearing down a drugstore. He sold us 110 full size 2" x 12" x 16' planks which he removed from the foundation, and delivered them to my grandmother's farm in Douglas. He charged us $2.50 apiece, delivered. New they would have cost $8.00 each. They were used for our foundation, to connect eight poles in a row, and for floor joists. Unloading and storing them in the cellar of a shed took a whole evening. With the foundation poles, floor joists and building permits in hand we had nothing to do but wait for good weather.

The first Saturday in March 1971, six poles were loaded on the trailer and Dad and I hauled them to Saquish. To get the poles lined up right was a major effort. Dad had a welder at his construction site take the circle from a basketball rim and weld a one foot piece of metal around the inside of the rim. He then took a 3' x 3' piece of 3/4" plywood and cut a circular hole in the center of the plywood so that the metal could just pass through.

The basketball rim would rest on the plywood. This was the template used to dig the holes for the foundation poles. It would stop the soft sand from collapsing. One foot below the surface the sand was moist and hard.

Most weekends we slept in Gene's cottage. When the weather warmed we sometimes slept in the SUV with our dog Jake. During the first weekend, the cottage was cold and damp after being closed without heat all Winter. We froze that night and experienced little sleep, but it was better than sleeping outside in the SUV. The next morning we started to build the foundation.

Before starting this project, we had bought a hand auger that was adjustable to dig a hole up to 15″ wide. Dad made two pipe extensions that would allow the 6′ long auger to dig 15′ down into the ground. Each extension was 5′ long and would screw on to the auger once the handle was removed. The handle was then reassembled. The template was set in the ground and the first couple of feet were dug by hand. Then the auger was used the rest of the way. You would stand on the plywood sheet that was part of the template, then the auger was placed in the hole and was turned enough times to fill it with sand. It was then lifted out of the hole and a release catch allowed you to empty it on the ground. This process was then repeated until the hole was 5′ deep.

Once there the handle was removed from the auger, a 5′ extension was attached and you were ready to go for another five feet. The digging process continued until wet sand came up in the auger. When this happened you stopped, took a deep breath and smiled. In only three or four more lifts you would bring up thick mud, and the digging process for that hole would be complete. After the first hole was completed you only had twenty-three more holes to dig and that would finish this part of the foundation project.

The shallowest hole we dug was 5′ and was located in back of the cottage. The deepest was over 10' and was in the front, near the beach. When the hole was over 5′ deep, lifting the auger was like pulling up the anchor on a boat. You used the hand over hand technique, and the deeper it was the more stress it put on you to pull it up.

The digging went fairly well until you hit a rock or other large object and the auger would dig no further. Since the poles would be placed exactly 8' apart, to properly carry the double planks that were used to complete the foundation, you had to work your way through any obstruction. Each time one was hit, you would tilt the auger at an angle and try to loosen the sand on the side of the object. If the object was small, after probing it for a minute or two, you could bring it up with the auger. If it was a big object, it was a different problem.

There were times we had to use an extended one half inch steel rod, long crowbar or other appropriate device, along with the auger, to scrape the embedded sand away from the object and create room to move it sidewards away from the hole. The deeper down the object was, the harder it was to move.

There were a couple of times, after working on the removal process for almost an hour with no success, we stopped and discussed what we might do next. One of our options was to remove the template, use shovels to make the hole much wider and dig a trench from the surface down to the embedded object, which in both cases turned out to be decent size stones. This would allow one of us to slide down the trench and do whatever was necessary to remove the embedded stone. The second option was to keep digging and probing for an additional fifteen minutes and if not successful, implement option one. In both instances we were successful with continuing to do what we were doing, but one time we were ready to quit when we noticed that the large stone had moved just a little. From our previous experience, we knew that when this happened, it was just a matter of time before you could move enough sand to wedge the stone away from the hole and keep digging. Never did we have to widen the hole and dig the trench. With no previous experience, on the morning after the freezing night, we started to dig the first hole.

After digging each hole the two of us, using the antique ice tongs, would drag a pole to the template, raise the pole to a vertical position on the plywood sheet. It was then maneuvered until three- quarters of the pole was over the open basketball rim and one-quarter was still on the plywood sheet.

One of us would then steady the pole while the other took a sledge hammer and on a count of three rapped the pole on the bottom and knocked it into the open hole. When the pole hit the mud it would sink in a couple of inches and then would not go any deeper, even when the weight of the cottage and furnishings were later placed on it. Who ever held the pole would guide it so that it landed close to where we wanted it. The pair of ice tongues were then used to twist and adjust the pole to its final position. Piano wire, which could be pulled very tight with no snag, was used to square the four foundation corner poles and to establish each row in a perfect line. Easier said than done! We put in three rows of eight poles with the poles spaced eight feet apart. The rows were spaced twelve feet between them. The railroad ties were used in the center row. We figured that if the poles ever needed replacing, the center row would be the hardest to do and the railroad ties would last the longest. It wasn't until twenty-five years later that this decision turned out to be a lifesaver.

That first weekend, working all day Saturday and Sunday, we placed the four corner poles. For the next four weeks we transported the rest of the poles and completed this part of the foundation. During this time we could see a major problem that was going to confront us. The 110 planks stored in Douglas, were the next items we would need to complete the foundation and move on to install the floor joists. Each plank weighed about 100 pounds. When we had initially weighed a number of them, they varied from 80 to 120 pounds. The boat trailer could carry 800 pounds. That's over twelve trips if we used the boat trailer to carry them, and would take three months time. That was way beyond our initial objective to finish the exterior by the 4th of July week end.

One of Dad's construction friends had a five ton heavy duty dump truck, but not a 4-wheel drive. We made an agreement with him to deliver the planks to Saquish for $50, a trip of over seventy- five miles each way. Remember this was back in 1971 when things were cheap by comparison.

There was a weekend in mid April that had a very low tide, early on a Saturday morning. That Friday evening we met Dad's friend at my grandmother's farm in Douglas. We loaded the 110 planks, weighing more than five tons, onto the truck and the driver headed to Saquish. That night he slept in his truck at the Duxbury Beach parking lot.

Dad and I slept at home but left early Saturday morning and arrived in Duxbury about 6:00 A.M. With the truck following us, we crossed over the bridge and went straight onto Duxbury Beach. The beach was as hard as a rock all the way to the crossover we wanted to use, which was right after High Pines. This crossover had the slight incline through about 30' of rocks, which that morning were damp and slippery.

About three quarters of the way through, the truck bogged down and was not able to move forward. It was, however, able to back down onto the beach. Two of the planks were removed from the truck and were placed in the track where the truck had bogged down. With a fast start it made the run onto the planks and over the slippery rocks and reached the back road. At Saquish the planks were dumped in front of our lot as close to the sand dunes as possible. The driver then returned home. He would have no problem going through the slippery rocks, because it was all downhill going.

It was now about 8:00 A.M. and we started to carry the planks up the soft, sandy dunes and stacked them near the foundation poles. We would each lift the same plank, put it on one of our shoulders and start walking up the steep sandy incline. After we moved the first plank, and with only 109 left to go, we decided to alternate who would walk in front and who would walk behind. It was questionable what position was the toughest, but when you were doing it they were both tough.

Your foot would dig in and slide a little after each step you took while climbing the sand dune. Ten hours later, about 6:00 P.M. the last plank was moved. Exhausted, we ate a sandwich for dinner and went to sleep.

The next morning both of us were sore and stiff as a board. We installed the last of the foundation poles and left early. We had a two hour drive home and were so exhausted that when we arrived at home we went straight to bed and slept for over twelve hours. The next day we were stiffer yet. You think a marathon is bad, it only lasts for a few short hours. This was more like training for the Navy Seals.

The following weekend we borrowed a transit and continued to Saquish. Between my Sophomore and Junior years in college, I had worked for the Worcester County Engineers and was familiar with using a transit. It was used to mark all the poles at the same vertical height, which we had determined to be the best height for the cottage foundation.

The 5' long two man hand saw was then used to cut all 24 poles to the same height that was marked using the transit. The saw was then used again to cut a 10' deep x 4' wide notch in each of the poles. This would then support two 2' x 12' x 16' planks which would lock in the 56' long foundation rows from front to back. Once the planks were put in place, a hand drill with a 3/4' drill bit was used to drill a hole through the two planks and the notched pole. The 10' long galvanized bolts along with the washers and the nuts which we had acquired when collecting the poles, were used to lock the planks and poles together. This made for a very solid foundation. It might not have been as strong as one made out of concrete or cinder blocks, but for a cottage on a remote beach, it was substantial.

One weekend during this time we brought Jake, our short haired English Pointer, with us. From then on he came with us every weekend. When Jake left the car, he saw a flock of seagulls on the beach near the curve. He took off and ran toward them. When he reached them they up and flew to the other end of the beach, a distance well over a mile. He ran after them again. Jake and the seagulls repeated this sequence one more time. He then attempted to drink the ocean dry and within one hour was as sick as a "dog." Jake also repeated this total scenario the next day, and after getting sick again, it was the last time he drank seawater.

The next weekend Mel Dorey and a friend were staying in Mel's cottage which was diagonally behind ours. Mel already had a cottage at Saquish for two years and he had a big Golden Retriever who thought he was King of the Beach.

On Saturday morning the dogs started a major fight which moved up on top of the 16' long planks we had stacked in front of our lot.

One dog would knock the other off the planks and would jump on top of him. This process was repeated three of four times, just like playing King of the Mountain, before we could break up the fight. It ended in a draw, with both dogs beaten up and having a number of cuts and bruises. The dogs never fought again, but neither one would go into the others territory. Territorial rights!

Approximately seventy planks were used for the floor joists. They extended twenty-four feet across the three foundation rows and overlapped an additional three feet on each side for the walkways. We used about three hundred 4" long galvanized spikes driven with a large ball penn hammer to lock them into the foundation.

Early on Sunday, after working all day Saturday swinging the hammer, our hands were numb. By that time you needed two hands to steady the hammer. When mid-afternoon arrived it was impossible to hit the spike straight, so we packed up and left for home.

I made a deal to buy our building materials from Village Lumber in Westboro. They had the overall best price in the local area and agreed to give me an additional 10% discount. They also delivered everything to our home at no extra charge. The first delivery was one thousand square feet of ¾" x 8"x 16' boards, which we used for the sub-flooring. Ann painted the boards in the garage, using two coats of Cupernal Wood Preservative Stain on both sides, which has kept them free from wood rot. This was the equivalent of painting a wall that was 10' high by 400' long but she did it without even using a step ladder, just saw horses. The last weekend in April we brought the sub-floor boards to Saquish and started to install them. Village Lumber then delivered a load of 2' x 4' x 8'-16' lumber, which we used for studding the building and making the trusses for the roof.

At this time our work accelerated. We would take Monday night to relax and then work Tuesday, Wednesday and Thursday night in my cellar, doing as much pre-cutting and assembling as possible. After work was finished on Thursday, we loaded the trailer with the precut lumber. Besides maintaining this exhaustive activity, which lasted more than two months, we also had full time jobs which required more than forty hours a week, often much more. We had made a personal commitment to finish the exterior building in four months. This would make it livable for the 4th of July weekend. We did whatever was necessary to meet this commitment.

On Friday afternoons Ann would make our meals for Friday night through Sunday and pack them in a cooler. After work on Friday, Dad would pick up the boat trailer and Jake, drive to Hanover where I would meet him after taking the express bus from Boston. We then continued to Saquish.

Since there was no commercial electric service at Saquish, we used my garage and cellar in Westboro to do as much pre-construction work as possible. At that time, all of our discretionary money was spent in buying building materials, so we couldn't afford to buy a gas driven electric generator. For the next year and one half all the work done at the beach was done by hand. Using the 3/4" hand drill to drill through the telephone poles and foundation timbers was tough, but using a hand saw to cut the studs, plywood sheets, sub-floor planks and Texture-111 was harder and took a lot more time. Just before Uncle Ted came from Florida to build our kitchen cabinets, we finally bought a gas driven electric generator. In the meantime, we had really paid the price of our initial generator decision, but that's life.

Our garage was 24' wide and had a 2' x 4' truss roof, the exact size of the trusses we needed for the cottage. I made a template in the cellar and we used it to pre-assemble the trusses and stored them until they were needed.

Ann and my anniversary was during the first weekend in May, so I didn't go to Saquish, but stayed home and celebrated with Ann. We even drank a champagne cocktail or two.

The next weekend we started to transport the sub-floor boards and 2' x 4' studs. On Sunday morning Ann, Kathi, Lorri and my mother drove to Duxbury and parked the car behind Prince's Garage. I drove out and met them. At that time Kathi had just turned five and Lorri was two and a half. It was a beautiful day, but after playing on the beach for a while, they wanted to help with the construction.

They each had a hammer and I would start some nails in the sub-flooring. They would then try to bang them in the rest of the way. Every now and then they were successful. For the rest of May and June, every Sunday the girls would come to Duxbury and I would drive out and meet them. We rented a parking spot at Prince's Garage and kept it until Dad bought a Jeep.

The next major problem was acquiring and then transporting all the building materials. This included buying forty sheets of Texture-111 for the siding, along with forty sheets of plywood and shingles for the roof. Next were the windows and doors. Then we had to transport all of them to the beach, including the 2'x 4' trusses for the roof. There were a few times that I took an early morning, before work, trip to the beach just to deliver a trailer load of material.

For the next number of weeks construction moved very fast. The sub-floor was completed, the trusses were assembled and stacked on the sub-floor and the cottage was framed. On the first weekend in June, Ann started to paint the Texture-111 plywood sheets at Saquish, giving each two coats of gray Cupernal Stain.

Stanley Bien, Goose Gosselin and Gene Wojnar were all experienced carpenters. Whenever advice or help was needed they would pitch right in. One Saturday they told us how to install the trusses and promised to help us that evening, after returning from Mass in Duxbury. Dad and I did the prep work, and after they returned the five of us had the twenty-one trusses installed in a couple hours time. The next morning we started installing the Texture-111. This was then followed by the windows and doors. Over the next couple of weeks the carpenters joined us to install the plywood and shingles for the roof.

It was now the 4th of July weekend and on that Saturday we completed the outside construction except for the porches and side walkways. We decided to stop working and enjoy the Summer, deferring all future projects till after Labor Day.

INITIAL CONSTRUCTION

CHAPTER 4

THE FIRST SUMMER

On Saturday morning of the 4th of July weekend 1971, I met my family at Prince's Garage. They brought sleeping bags, pillows, plates, cups, silverware, basic food supplies, a Coleman stove and a host of other items to make living on a remote beach practical.

Stanley Bien had a spare propane gas refrigerator and a 100 pound propane gas bottle that he let us use. At the back corner of the building we used two sheets of plywood to make a semi-enclosed temporary bathroom.

Two gaslights were connected to the gas supply then coupled with two kerosene lanterns gave us the equivalent of 300-400 watts of light. Richard Balakier had drilled a well on our property, right near where we placed the backdoor, but he had stopped using it when we bought the land and started construction. We connected a hand pump to the well and had fresh water. With these basic necessities in place Ann, the girls and I decided to stay for the summer. A washbasin was used as a bathtub for Kathi and Lorri and as a sink for Ann and me. A Coleman stove was used to heat hot water and to cook.

During our initial construction in March-June, every time there was a major storm, lobster pots would wash onto the beach. It was not easy for the lobstermen to reach Saquish and reclaim their pots. Many were left there with most damaged beyond repair.

We had bought a 12' aluminum boat with a twelve horsepower motor and brought it to Saquish. So that Sunday we went fishing and caught many mackerel, which were excellent lobster bait. Then we prepared our lobster pots. The pots were made of wood and after staying out of the water and drying out, two or three good size rocks were placed in each pot to sink and hold them on the bottom. After three days the wood absorbed enough water to hold the bottom without the rocks. During this time, you supposedly could not catch lobsters. On Monday we put 10 pots into the water.

On Tuesday I drove to Hanover, took an express bus to Boston and went to work. Ann and the girls had their first day alone at the beach. I took the 5:00 p.m. express bus from Boston to Hanover, where my SUV was parked, and reached Saquish about 6:30. Ann had made a healthy meal for dinner, but before eating we went out to check the lobster pots.

To our surprise we had caught four good size lobsters. We brought them in and had them for dinner, disregarding the meal Ann had made. They were excellent and we decided to do the same thing the following afternoon. It turned out to be the complete opposite. No lobsters and no meal prepared so we made peanut butter and jelly sandwiches, a very good beach picnic, but not if you were anticipating lobsters for dinner.

On the Saturday of Labor Day weekend Ann, my Mother and a number of other women went to Marshfield on Goose's boat to dig clams. We were going to have a large clambake the next day. Upon returning they told us that a major hurricane would hit later that day.

In the early seventies we had limited communication with the outside world, especially with no electricity or telephone service available to us. The hurricane hit early that afternoon. With the high winds, our front wall was shaking and appeared ready to collapse. Dad and I retrieved some long two by four boards stored under the cottage and spiked them in at an angle between the floor and the studs in the front wall. This was sufficient to stop the front wall from collapsing and ruin a good part of the cottage we had worked so hard to build.

Before the hurricane hit I counted fifty-five boats on moorings in the front bay. Due to the heavy rain and breaking surf a number of boats filled with water. Some sank. Others broke their moorings and either were thrust out to sea by the hurricane winds and outgoing tide or were hurdled onto the beach by the breaking swells and incoming tide. Each time a boat was beached, a number of people each with a five gallon bucket, would alternate getting into the boat and bail it out. Quite often a large wave would come over the side and partially fill the boat again. With a small amount of water left in the boat, tow chains from two large trucks were attached to it. Foot by foot the boat was slowly dragged back to the dunes away from the crashing waves.

By dark the hurricane had passed. Six of the initial fifty-five boats were left on their moorings. The rest had either sunk, crashed on the rocks, washed out to sea or were thrust onto the beach. One of the remaining six boats was Richard Balakier's. The next morning his boat, over 20' long, had disappeared. Needless to say, we never had the clambake. About two weeks later, Richard received a call from the Plymouth Harbor Master. A large fishing boat located his boat floating in the open ocean somewhere East of Provincetown. The Coast Guard was notified and in turn notified the Plymouth Harbor Master. An amazing thing about this was that when Richard's boat was moored he had two fishing rods in holders extending out of the sides of his boat. When the boat was returned, the rods were still there, and no damage was done to the boat. Again that was back in 1971.

The Summer was spent fishing, clamming, lobstering, resting, relaxing and swimming. It was a wonderful Summer, the first time the girls had spent any time at the ocean. It reminded me of the time I'd spent at the ocean, when I was a little older than they were. We enjoyed all aspects of it. The quiet evenings with the full moon rising out of the ocean, the walks on the often deserted beach with our two young daughters, the collecting of sea glass and other treasures that the ocean brought in and picnics at the lighthouse were amongst other endeavors that were new to us. Collecting sea glass and picnics at the Gurnet Light continued to be highlights for our children and then grandchildren for the forty years. Now, however it was time to return home so Kathi could start Kindergarten. We couldn't wait for next year.

In September and October 1971, Dad and I installed a permanent floor and starting construction on a 8' x 12' shed underneath the cottage. We brought in 30 sheets of ¾" exterior plywood for the floor, a host of 2" x 8" planks for the porches and a number of two by fours to start studding the interior. A gas stove and a gas refrigerator were also brought to the cottage. As we started to work on the interior, the amount of time to finish each project expanded considerably. Dad and I still made time for lobstering and a little striped bass fishing, but work on the cottage was our focus.

The hunting season started on October 20 so on October 15 we made our last trip to Saquish for the year, with work to resume the following Spring. Again we couldn't wait for it to arrive.

GURNET LIGHT

CHAPTER 5

FINISHING CONSTRUCTION

Over the next few years we would work on finishing construction from early March through June and after Labor Day through mid-October.

We started again in March 1972. For the first project we installed a kerosene stove that my parents had used in their home when they were first married. It provided enough heat for the cottage until 1994.

When we started to work, Uncle Stan came with us along with our dog Jake. Uncle Stan had married my mother's sister Josie. After their marriage he was involved in a motor cycle accident and received severe head injuries. Because of the injuries, the amount of work he could do was limited and he would talk only when it was required. Working with us provided an outlet he enjoyed, plus it added an extra pair of hands during construction.

There were a couple of incidents that disturbed Dad and me, but looking back they were rather humorous. The first was on a Saturday evening when we were working on the shed. We asked Stan to start dinner. Once it was ready we'd join him. Three steaks were normally prepared for our Saturday night dinner. A while later we went into the cottage to see what was taking so long. There sat Stan eating his last bite of steak. Stan said, "Gee, I was wondering when you guys were going to come in and eat your steaks, I already finished mine." By then ours were cold.

The next weekend we again asked Stan to prepare dinner and just before he placed the steaks in the frying pan to come and let us know. About twenty minutes went by and Stan came out of the cottage and told us everything was ready and he was going to fry the steaks. We told him to start and we would be there in a couple of minutes. He went into the cottage, came back out and said, "Jake has eaten two of the steaks. I placed the three steaks on a plate near the stove. When I went outside to tell you I was ready Jake ate two steaks. I was able to pry the third one away from him."

Lessons learned, don't let Jake stay in the cottage alone when you're preparing steaks. Be specific and cautious when Stan is doing anything. With this in mind, we enjoyed Stan and the time he spent with us. He was a great helper and had an enjoyable time.

Over the next number of weeks we finished the shed and partitioned all the rooms with studs. Then Dad started to work on the gas and plumbing lines. I wired the cottage in case electricity was available in the future. At the end of May I met the electrical inspector at Powder Point Bridge and brought him to Saquish. Our first building inspection passed.

We had to make a major decision regarding what material to use for the walls. Ann wanted Knotty Pine tongue and grove boards. Dad and I thought that one-quarter inch paneling would be less expensive and easier to install. Village Lumber gave us a price per square foot for the Knotty Pine that was less expensive than the price for paneling. Knotty Pine was used for the walls and ceilings. Ann was happy.

In mid-October, 1972 Uncle Ted and Aunt Ann came from Florida and spent two weeks at Saquish with my parents. Years before, Dad did the plumbing for Ted when he built his first house. Uncle Ted, who was an excellent carpenter for finish work, was returning the favor by building our kitchen cabinets using Knotty Pine boards. My Uncle Chet gave us an old table saw and we bought a small gas generator for electrical power which we would later use to pump our water into a pressurized tank.

Ted and Ann loved lobster and Dad had promised them he would catch all they could eat. The year before we had lobstered till mid-October and were doing quite well. As fate would have it, they did not catch one lobster during the two week process. However the cabinets that Ted designed and built turned out to be beautiful, a dream kitchen for Ann.

The inside finish work took substantially longer than constructing the exterior building. The next three Springs and Falls were spent finishing the porch with 2" x 8" boards, installing the septic system and completing the Knotty Pine finish in all the rooms. Aunt Josie and my mother were also coming to Saquish in the Spring and Fall. Josie and I spent many weekends measuring, cutting and nailing well over 700 pieces of Knotty Pine board to finish the inside of the cottage. In the Spring of 1975, we built two closets in the bedrooms and installed louver doors on all the closets in the bedrooms, hallway and bathrooms. Dad was able to acquire some surplus pine boards from one of his construction jobs. They were used to complete the attic floor.

Gas lights were installed each time we finished an area with Knotty Pine boards. A double light was over the kitchen table and two were on the den walls. One was over the kitchen sink and one was in the hallway and each of the bathrooms. The girls bedroom had two and my parents and our bedrooms had one. When they were all turned on, the cottage lit up like a Christmas tree. When we arrived to work on the Friday evening of a cold spring weekend, we no longer had to use the construction heater to deal with the chill. We would simply light the twelve gas lights, turn on the four burners on the gas stove and presto, the chill would be gone.

What a few years before was a 24′ x 40′ single room with a temporary bathroom was transformed. It now was a finished cottage with a combination kitchen and den, three bedrooms, two bathrooms and seven closets. This finished our major construction until 1994. Then we added a second floor observation room, our "Impossible Dream."

From the time we had first started construction until we finished it, over thirty tons of material and furnishings were transported to our cottage at Saquish. Outside of the five tons initially hauled by the leased pick up truck and driver, the rest of it was hauled by the boat trailer and SUV. Loading and unloading everything was a good way to stay in shape.

There were two events that occurred during our finishing the construction, that are worth mentioning. On a cold Friday evening in March, after an extreme high tide, the marsh in the lowlands between The Gurnet and Saquish was frozen. On that dark, cold night we continued on what I thought was the road when all of a sudden we crashed through the ice and bogged down in the marsh. We saw a light in a house at The Gurnet, so we left the SUV, sloshed through the ice and mud and went to get help. A home owner, who lived at The Gurnet was there, and he came down to the frozen marsh with his large pickup truck and with a long chain pulled us out. We then circled The Gurnet using the narrow cart paths and came around through the Boat Hole access area. We had a large construction heater at the cottage which we used to warm up and dry out our clothes, including my business suit and shoes. The construction heater had proven to be very effective in heating the cottage on cold Friday nights in the early Spring, as we were finishing the inside work and before we had the gas lights.

The second event occurred when I was unable to go for a weekend, so Dad and Stan went alone. Dad had little experience in driving the 4WD and on Friday night they bogged down in the ball bearing rock crossover beyond High Pines. The weather was terrible that night and no one else came to Saquish. They were unable to get the vehicle out of the ball bearing rocks and had to spend the night sleeping in the SUV. The next morning one of our friends was able to pull them free. Dad never mentioned this. One day I met the friend on the beach and he told me what happened. I never said anything to Dad about this and he never said anything either, but I hoped they had a good nights sleep!

CHAPTER 6

GROWING UP

When we started to build in March 1971 Kathi was four years old and Lorri was two. They were affectionately called "The Girls."

One of the first things they did was to name the cottage that we were building "The Campy." It was called that until we added the second floor addition in 1994.

The first Summer they became involved in clamming, flounder fishing and lobstering. Every Friday they would go with Ann to gather razor clams for flounder bait, and then awaited my return from work. When I arrived we would hop in the boat, catch enough flounders to bait the pots, pull them and return with enough lobsters for dinner. One Friday Lorri sliced her finger on a razor clam and was taken to Jordan Hospital in Plymouth for stitches. There was no more clamming, flounder fishing or lobstering that day.

On weekends and vacations, flounder fishing and lobstering were two of our more frequent events. Kathi couldn't wait to go fishing until it was time to go. Then she would change her mind. She also couldn't wait until she was old enough to get her own lobster license and pots. Once she was old enough, another mind change. She was the same about clamming, at first wanting to go, then again changing her mind.

When flounder fishing the girls would use hand lines held over the side of the boat. I would bait the hooks and take off the fish. When lobstering they liked to record, by date, the number of lobsters we caught in each individual pot. They used a wooden board and pencil to do this. At the end of the season we would count the number of lobsters caught in each pot and then come up with the total for the season. This proved very helpful in filing my annual report with the state, while also remembering that the girls enjoyed writing down the numbers. They were happy when we caught many lobsters and disappointed when we didn't catch any.

One day when we were anchored flounder fishing by the Bell, with more than ten other boats nearby, a large shark with its fin above the water swam by us and the other boats, and kept circling around. Our boat was only twelve feet long, and the shark appeared just as long. The other boats all pulled up their anchors, started their engines and left.

Ann and the girls wanted to leave, but I didn't want to attract its attention. We waited until the large shark swam away. My three girls were petrified so we quickly headed for shore. The next time we decided to go flounder fishing, the girls were very reluctant.

However they stood up to the challenge. When they started to catch flounder any thoughts of sharks disappeared.

Lorri really liked to go flounder fishing, but didn't have a long attention span while she was doing it. One day my father, the girl's grandfather (Dziadziu in Polish) was taking care of Lorri and decided to take her fishing. They were anchored by the Bell with Lorri sitting in the front of the boat looking at Dziadziu and watching the tide run out. She wore a life preserver and bored with fishing, she was trying to catch the seaweed and everything else in the water that was rushing by the boat with the outgoing tide. All at once she reached too far and fell out of the boat, yelled and was rapidly carried by the fast moving tide. Dziadziu reached out and grabbed her arm as she was about to be swept by him, pulled her tight to the boat and held her in the water until she regained her composure. They then returned to shore. Lorri took a warm shower and then Dziadziu told her they had to go back fishing. Lorri did not want to go. Dziadziu assured her that if she immediately went back out in the boat, she would never have fears of being in a boat again. She reluctantly went and what she was told turned out to be true.

The girls made many friends. Kathi's best friends were Susan Wojnar and Susan Pink. Lorri's was Tammie Pink. While I was commuting to Boston by way of the express bus, Ann and the girls would drive me to Hanover once a week, shop all day, pick me up at 6:00 P.M. and return to the beach. They would do the food shopping for the next week. Then they would go to a second hand clothing store and buy some extra small women's clothes and high heel shoes. For the rest of the week, the girls and their friends would develop a multi-act play. They had many costume changes using the clothes they had purchased. During the weekend, when parents were at Saquish, the girls would put on the play in our den and use their bedroom for changing costumes between acts.

We had a small black and white television that ran off a car battery. On weekdays at 3:00 P.M., the girls and their friends would gather around our battery operated T.V. and watch General Hospital. Our cottage was a major location to host many of the social activities for the young girls that spent their Summers at the beach.

The Gurnet Saquish Association provided an instructor one morning a week, to teach Arts and Crafts or provide swimming lessons for the children. Both of our girls would freeze each time they took a swimming lesson, but they both learned how to swim. At Arts and Crafts, Kathi's favorite activity was making items with colored sand. As a follow up to their swimming lessons, each year right after Christmas, we would go to Saquish and stay for a couple of days. From there we would go to Dunfey's Hyannis Resort for the rest of the week. Dunfey's had a large heated pool which the girls enjoyed. During the week immediately following Christmas, there were few people that stayed at Dunfey's. There were many times that we had the pool all to ourselves. The girls also improved their swimming abilities at Dunfey's.

When Kathi's first baby tooth was loose she couldn't wait for it to come out. She was going to put it under her pillow and hoped to receive some money from the Tooth Fairy. One day we went to Western Point to play on the rocks and she kept wiggling her loose tooth. She was warned, to no avail, not to do that. It finally came out and she dropped it. The tooth disappeared amongst the large rocks, small pebbles and sand. We searched and searched but couldn't find it.

Kathi was very upset and started to cry. We offered to help her write a note to the Tooth Fairy explaining what happened, then she could place it under her pillow and that night something good might take place. Sure enough, the next morning the note was gone and there was a $1 dollar bill under the pillow. It's amazing what can happen if you believe in something and take the time to tell the truth.

On the 4th of July, 1976 the people of Saquish had a Bicentennial Parade that went from one end of Saquish Beach to the other and then back again. The girls and their friends made Indian costumes. They painted a sheet and constructed a teepee for their float in the parade. The parade was such a success that there has been one every 4th of July since then. We have worn multiple costumes with different ones almost every year. The girls and then our grandchildren have participated in the parade every time they were at Saquish on that date. On the 4th of July, 2010 we had our thirty-fifth annual parade. Ann, Kathi, her husband Franz, Sydney, Michael, Max, and I all dressed as Hawaiians and led the parade. Lorri watched the parade while taking pictures. She is our family photographer.

During the first Saquish talent show, the girls and their friends all danced to the song "Under Cover Angel" and were a smashing hit. However none of them went on to become famous singers, dancers or actresses. It's a long way from being a success in a small community to making it in the big time.

At dinner time Ann would go out on the porch and ring a loud bell that was the signal for the girls to come home for dinner and it worked. After dinner the girls, had the chore of doing the dinner dishes. Every now and then they would do a little grousing, but in general, they accepted it as their responsibility.

Quite often my mother, their grandmother (Babciu in Polish) would tell them to go out to play and she would do the dishes for them. Ann and I would get upset because it made us look like the bad guys in forcing the girls to do the chore. We looked at this as something a typical grandparent might do, spoil the grandchildren. Its amazing how looking back on something can change your perception. We now believe that a grandparent should be able to do something for a grandchild as long as it did not break any major rule or do any harm. When Babciu did this, it made her feel good and the girls were absolutely pleased. They still knew that the next night and until Babciu did it for them again, it was still their chore to do the dinner dishes.

During the Summer, Ann required the girls to read a book for one hour a day. If they didn't finish their reading before dinner, then after doing the dishes they had to do their reading before going out to play with their friends. They soon learned to read in the afternoon.

One of the family activities that we all enjoyed was collecting beach glass during low tides. Beach glass is glass that has washed in from the ocean and was deposited on the beach. The moving water and sand polishes the glass until there are no sharp edges. Therefore you cannot cut yourself. This is our definition of beach glass.

Beach glass comes in many colors. The rarest is red, which comes from old cars that had red glass tail lights, hand lanterns and old sea buoys used as channel markers. The second rarest is blue and is the prize everyone looks for. Any time that Ann and I walked the beach in the late afternoon we always had a bet. If either one of us found a piece of blue sea glass, the other person had to make dinner that evening. Ann won the bet more often than I did. Our two daughters and four grandchildren enjoyed finding any color. Green, brown and white are the most common and are easier to find. We spent many hours walking the beach collecting beach glass and everyone loved doing it. With plastic replacing glass bottles, however, the amount of beach glass has decreased. You just have to spend more time looking and be willing to find fewer pieces. The peaceful, quite walk and enjoyment still remains the same.

Picnics at the lighthouse on The Gurnet were another big hit. They were frequent yet special. On a clear day, you could look eighteen miles across Cape Cod Bay and see the sand dunes and tower at Provincetown. When our grandchildren were at Saquish, they always had to go to the lighthouse for a picnic.

Once when Lorri, Cory and Sydney were at Saquish for a weekend, Monday morning came and they had not been to the lighthouse. Cory insisted that I take him there while his mother packed the SUV. When we reached the lighthouse, two Coast Guard men from their Scituate location were repairing the light. Lightning had struck the lighthouse over the weekend and disabled it and they had come from Scituate to repair it. Cory asked them if he could go inside. They were delighted to show a young boy the inside of their lighthouse and they gave us a private tour. We started at the bottom and using a spiral staircase worked our way to the top. The view of Provincetown was spectacular. It was like looking at the large sand dunes and tower, that were eighteen miles across the bay, with a magnifying glass. Cory's weekend was made.

At the lighthouse Sydney enjoyed climbing the apple tree and would climb a little higher each time she came to visit us. She took after her mother Lorri who enjoyed going to the lighthouse when she was young. One day Lorri said, "I don't remember the apple tree when I was little." Ann replied, "When you were a little girl the apple tree was just a seedling." Its amazing as you get older how things change.

Michael and Max were staying with us while Kathi and Franz were vacationing in Boston. The activity Michael wanted to do the most was go back for a second picnic at the lighthouse. He enjoyed standing on the flat area facing the steep grassy hill on which the lighthouse was built. There were numerous holes in the side of the hill made by moles. Every now and then one would come out and nibble on an apple that had dropped from the tree. Michael would pick up an apple, climb half way up the hill, and put the apple in front of a hole. He would then slide down the hill, on his rear end, get up on his feet, stand there like a statue and watch. When his brother Max, who was two years old, was asked if he wanted to go to the lighthouse with us, all he would say was "Me too." In Max talk that meant yes.

When Michael was two we bought a potty seat to toilet train him while at Saquish. It worked very well. Two years later his brother Max was two when they came. It was time to bring out the potty seat and start to train Max. When not used it was left beside the toilet up against the shower wall. One morning Michael went into the bathroom, shut the door and was using the toilet. All of a sudden he screamed, "Help Mimi help, I need help." Ann rushed into the bathroom and there sat Michael with the potty seat stuck over his head and his ears pinned back within it. He was in a state of panic.

It was so funny that Ann couldn't stop laughing, but she was able to calm Michael down by assuring him that she would help. First, however, she had to get a camera to take a picture. She then tried to remove the potty seat but wasn't successful. She needed help and went to the front door and yelled to

Michael's parents who were on the beach. Kathi and Franz came running and they along with Ann struggled for a few minutes. Then it came off. They all went into a fit of laughter. Along with having a good laugh, Michael learned a lesson that will last him a life time. Don't ever put your head into a toilet seat again. The next time there might not be anyone there to help.

Collecting wood for bonfires and toasting marshmallows for mores were also a big hit. That frequently was our nightly entertainment. We would sit around the bonfires, eat's mores and sing songs with the girls, their friends and finally our grandchildren. Ann had written a special song for each of our grandchildren when they were born, and when they were sitting around the bonfires, she had to sing their song to each one of them. Shortly after Max was born, Ann had written the words for his song but was struggling with the tune. Franz then kidded Ann about not having a song for Max, so he made up a rap song he named "Max has no song" and sang it to Ann. The next time Cory and Sydney were at a bonfire she told them about the song that Uncle Franz had written. They asked her to sing it and when she did they laughed so hard that they had her sing it again and again. Everyone memorized the words. Cory and Sydney then had Ann call California and when everyone there came to the phone, we all busted out and sang Max's temporary song. A smashing, laughing success.

When the girls were older they baby sat for Ricky, Ethan and Becky Balakier who lived next door. Each year we would take boat trips to Plymouth and Provincetown with them. One day when Ethan was a young boy, he was separated from us in the Provincetown Mall. We all went in different directions looking for him. A police officer had found him, and when Ethan saw me go by, he told the police officer, "I know that man." All's well that ends well.

When my sister Barbara, her husband Ken and their three boys John, Paul and Mike came to visit us we created an after dinner activity we called "Fun Night." Fun night consisted of a number of physical activities they all had to do. If successful they would receive a reward of a nickel, dime or quarter based on the toughness of the event.

The events included jumping around the table forward and backward, using only one leg, first with the right leg then with the left. This would be followed by walking on all fours, first forward then backward, for a defined distance. One of the toughest was hanging on to a 2"x 4" truss roof beam for one minute. The toughest of all was one that seemed very easy. It required laying on your back for five minutes without moving, opening your eyes or making any sound. This one had a fifty cent reward. It amazed us that young children had such a hard time doing this.

Fun night was created to help tire the young children before their bed time. It worked great! We had fun nights a number of times with Cory, Sydney and several other young children that have visited us. Every child that experienced the activity had a fun time and all the adults enjoyed it and had many laughs. It is interesting to see the difference in physical development of young children all at or about the same age.

On low tides Ann and the girls took long walks on the beach, often all the way around Western Point. Occasionally they would walk around The Gurnet. One day Ann took a can of paint and a paintbrush and both Kathi and Lorri each painted their name on a rock at Western Point. Ann has taken Cory, Sydney, Michael and Max to Western point and they each painted their names on a rock. It was interesting to see how long the names lasted before they were washed away by the sea. Everyone has enjoyed playing there, climbing the rocks and collecting treasures such as star fish and shells.

Easter time was special at Saquish. Aunt Joe and Uncle Stan would often join us and we would have large Easter dinners, and Easter egg hunts. One Easter my parents bought two bunnies for the girls. Early in the morning the bunnies were released inside the cottage. When the girls awoke they found them and were elated. On a subsequent Easter, Lorri was convinced that she had seen the Easter Bunny in her room when she awoke during the night. She said it was purple in color with big pink polka dots. She wholeheartedly believed this for a number of years. She might still believe it.

My dad had bought a large trap that could catch animals alive without hurting them. Each year I would set it and catch some small bunnies. When a bunny was caught, the girls and their friends would form a semicircle around the trap. Then it was released and they all tried to catch it. The bunnies were so fast that none of the children ever touched one.

Our grandchildren also enjoyed releasing small animals caught in the trap. Along with bunnies we would often catch small birds, mice, moles and voles. Michael and Max would wake up early and wait for me to wake up before going to check the trap. They were afraid of being attacked by whatever was in it. Max always carried a stick with him for protection. They never were attacked so the stick was never used. For spending a few hours in the trap, the animals received a very good meal. The menu included carrots, lettuce, bread, peanut butter and cheese. The choice was theirs.

We bought a secondhand double bed and two antique bureaus for the girls room. They became dissatisfied with the pale looking furniture and wanted to repaint it. Ann and I agreed that they could paint it and could chose their own colors. They chose lime green and hot pink, two very prevalent Key West colors. A few years later we replaced the double bed with a bunk bed set. The girls would then argue about who would sleep in the top bunk. Ann easily solved that problem. Whenever she washed the sheets they would change sleeping positions. Whoever had the top bunk would like to have gone weeks without having the sheets washed. Even our grandchildren would argue about who would sleep in the top bunk. That problem was left for their parents to resolve.

Playing in the tide pools was a fun activity. After the tide receded the girls could play for hours. It was astonishing how far the ocean receded on an extra low tide, leaving the pools and the exposed beach behind. It was also an excellent time to gather sand dollars. After drying them in the sun, they were soaked in bleach and water and then they were dried in the sun again. Later, Ann and the girls would create Christmas ornaments with them.

One year, Ann's father built the girls a 6′ x 6′ yellow raft. It was made of boards and 8″ of Styrofoam was used for flotation. The girls and their friends enjoyed it for many years. They moved the anchor in and out with the flow of the tide and the raft would follow. During the winter it was stored under the cottage.

Ann's mother loved to come to Saquish and spend time with the girls. She crocheted matching outfits for them. She also crocheted them twin bedspreads for the new bunk beds we had bought for their room. Every time she came she brought a new crocheted item and the girls would get so excited. Her time was limited though, because Ann's father could not wait to go home and take care of his large garden. One of the by products of the garden was that Ann's mother would pickle a large amount of green tomatoes. This was one of my favorite appetizers, before dinner, as they go well with a real cold beer. Just as she brought the girls something they really liked, I really liked the pickled green tomatoes. However, I didn't jump up and down to show my pleasure. I left that activity to the girls!

Ann's sister Dot had a family of eight children and she was an excellent cook. After her husband Tom passed away she would often come to the cottage to spend time with us. She like Ann's mother, always brought goodies that the girls and I enjoyed. Of the many goodies she brought two of our favorites were pumpkin and banana bread, really tasty in the morning for breakfast.

Each Fall we would take my father's Jeep and gather seaweed from the back bay and spread it on the sand dunes in front of the cottage. When Kathi was eleven she was taught how to drive the Jeep on the beach. One day we gathered a load of seaweed and backed the Jeep up to the steps in front of the cottage. After unloading the seaweed, Ann asked Kathi to drive the Jeep back to the beach. She climbed in, started the Jeep, mistakenly put it in reverse and backed into the steps.

The steps were nearly wiped out and substantial damage was done to the back of the Jeep. Her first driving accident and she was nowhere near old enough to have a driver's license. Her friends then renamed her "Crash Matuzek." She had the chance to continue on and become the first woman to race in the Daytona 500, but never pursued that opportunity. I guess one accident was enough.

Since the girls were getting old enough to drive on the beach, they were also old enough to start taking on another major responsibility. With the ocean just about surrounding the cottage the severe winter weather impacted the stained wood on the cottage sides, the porches, the side walk ways and the hand rails. Every couple of years we had to wash all of them down with a mold remover and give them a fresh coat of stain. Now the girls could help us with this project, and a couple of years later did most of the staining all by themselves. Fortunately or unfortunately, with age comes responsibility.

One time Ann found the wrappings from a freshly opened cigarette package on Dziadziu's bureau. He was back home for the week. She didn't say anything until that evening at dinner. She then showed the girls what she found and asked, "Who did it?" Lorri immediately turned as red as a beet and Kathi said. "It wasn't me." Lorri then admitted that she took a pack of cigarettes from Dziadziu's closet and that she and Tammie smoked some.

Lorri's punishment was to tell Dziadziu what she had done and apologize when he returned the next weekend. Lorri dreaded telling him and asked for any other punishment, even being grounded for two weeks. Ann did not change her mind. When the weekend came, Dziadziu calmly listened, told her it was wrong, asked her why she did it and then accepted her apology. A real lesson learned.

There was a place in the sand dunes called "The Pit" where Lorri and her friends would meet, talk, and play some games. Kathi and her friends would do the same in Pink's Loft. The older kids had parties at The Curve, where there was liquor available, so the girls were not allowed to go there.

One Friday evening Ann and I went by the Curve on our evening walk and saw Kathi and her friends. She was grounded for the following night when her friends had planned a party.

The following day Lorri and Susan helped her develop a plan to attend the party. They removed the screen from the small bedroom window that overlooked the back porch. They then moved the picnic table so it was under the window. A trial run was done and the opening was just big enough for Kathi to squeeze through with help from Lorri. They did this on Saturday afternoon when Ann was out for her daily walk and I was lobstering.

That evening Kathi told us that she was going to bed very early. She went into the bedroom and instead of going to sleep, she packed her bed with pillows and covered them with blankets to look like she was sleeping. A little later as Lorri was going out, she turned and went back to the bedroom to find something she had supposedly forgot. She then helped Kathi get up and through the window. Susan was on the back porch and helped Kathi, who was coming out head first, get out and onto the table without making any noise. Lorri put the screen back in the window, came out said, "Goodbye" and left. When Lorri came home that evening, the whole process was done in reverse, and was done to perfection. We never knew anything about this until years later when we had a "Green Light" session. A green light session was when you could tell anything you had done more than two years in the past and there would be no repercussions. As the girls matured we had a number of these sessions with them and Susan. We all had some good laughs.

When Kathi and Susan were in their teens, my mother gave them advice on how to attract boys. One Summer they both had boy friends that lived on Clark's Island. The boys had a small boat and rowed back and forth to Saquish. Didn't know how good the advice was, but the romances didn't last long.

A couple of years later, my mother passed away. She developed breast cancer ten years before and it then reoccurred. After her chemotherapy treatment, she and my father would go to Saquish. For the next week she would be sick. While at Saquish recuperating she would relax and have peace of mind while enjoying the environment. She loved her grandchildren and would do anything to make them happy. Unfortunately her time at Saquish lasted less than ten years, but they were very enjoyable ones.

One Saturday night Ann and I went to the Balakier's to play cards. Kathi wanted to stay home and have some friends over. We told her O.K. but no boys. Midway through the evening, I had to come back to get an item I had left in the cottage. A couple of their boyfriends were there with Kathi and her friends. When they heard me coming up the stairs they had the boys hide in the small shower in our bathroom. When I entered the cottage the girls appeared to be on edge and uneasy. However, I picked up the item then proceeded to use the bathroom. The boys, who were hiding in the shower about one foot away from me, were scared stiff. After finishing, I returned to the Balakier's and the boys immediately went out the back door. No more games that evening. This was another story told during one of our "Green Light" sessions.

Anytime Ann needed a sign she always asked Kathi to paint it. Ann was convinced Kathi was better at printing than she was. Kathi made signs for the church, raffles, items for sale by our beach association, our personal for sale items and for free items that we would leave in front of the cottage.

Anything left there would disappear immediately.

When we were building the cottage, Dad worked at a construction site remodeling a large hospital. He was able to acquire a lab sink with two basins. One was regular size, the other was deep. The girls and grandchildren all enjoyed taking a bath in the deep sink. They all called it the "Saquish Tubby." Our granddaughter Sydney loved it and enjoyed soaking in it as long as she could. One evening when dinner was ready she wanted to stay in the tubby. We put a tray over the normal sink and served her hot dogs and beans on a plate. She continued to soak while she enjoyed her meal. A memory that will last forever!

One major activity enjoyed by the grandchildren was jumping off the front porch and steps into the sand dune. When their mothers were young, the sand dunes were nowhere near as high, so this was an activity that was unique to the grandchildren.

Along with enjoying jumping off the porch into the sand dunes Max really enjoyed hitting plastic golf balls off the porch and into the dunes. He started at two years old and did very well. By the time he was three he hit them straight and for a decent distance. Reminded me of a famous golfer who was on the Ed Sullivan T.V. show at about that age. Who knows how good a golfer Max will turn out to be. With his Dad Franz as his instructor, you never know.

Each grandchild had his or her own surprise container located in the observation room. Every time they came to Saquish there was a new surprise. As soon as they arrived, they gave us a big hug and kiss, then ran up the stairs to find out what was in their container. To see their faces glow was a special treat. Cory had a chest, Sydney a basket, Michael a round box with a lighthouse picture on the cover and Max a rectangle box covered with shells.

As our daughters, matured their time at Saquish decreased. They entered high school, acquired summer jobs and played sports. From there it was on to college, grad school, professional careers, marriage and children. Each time Lorri and Kathi had the opportunities to come back to Saquish, they not only enjoyed reliving many of their past memories, but also enjoyed the present time. Their children Cory, Sydney, Michael and Max enjoyed many of the same activities that their mothers had enjoyed when they were young.

Growing up is quite an accomplishment.

THE GIRLS KATHI, ANN and LORRI

MICHAEL, SYDNEY, CORY and MAX

CHAPTER 7

THE IMPOSSIBLE DREAM

After we received our building permit in 1971, there were just a few cottages built by a developer, and then Plymouth stopped issuing permits for new construction. Plymouth allowed the building of second story additions for a period, but then stopped issuing those type of permits. The reasons given were that Saquish was a "wetlands" area and it did not have any town owned roads there or connected to it.

Ann had always wanted a second floor observation room to give us an elevated view of the ocean and the gorgeous surrounding area. In the Spring of 1992 while walking the back road, she noticed a cottage that had its roof re-shingled and raised enough to have a loft built inside.

Les Plimpton, a local builder who owned Scorpio Craftsmen, had a cottage near ours and had done the work. We talked with Les about adding a second story observation room. He said with the need to re-shingle coupled with some deteriorated roofing wood, they were able to acquire a permit for the reconstruction that also allowed a small loft to be built on the inside. For a reasonable fee, he would work with us to try to acquire the permits for our second story addition with no guarantee of success.

Les was well thought of by the people that worked in the town of Plymouth Building Departments. He was aware that a number of people who applied to build a second story had worked through all the permitting departments but were turned down by the Health Department, one of the last departments to sign off on the permit.

In late 1992, we signed a contract with Les to move forward. The first thing he did was to bring a number of the Conservation Committee members to Saquish where he explained what he wanted to do. He told them that when the roof was taken down he would walk the material to the back porch and deposit it in his large truck, then haul it to the dump. The material to build the second story addition would be handled in the same way, from truck to the back porch.

Nothing would ever touch the ground or sand dunes. With our agreeing to a few concessions they wanted, they gave us a verbal O.K.

Before we moved any further along the normal permitting process, Les wanted to have the O.K. from the Board of Health. Les felt that if they approved, the Building Department and the Planning Board approval would be achievable.

The Board of Health became a major issue. We met with the person in charge and he put a number of obstacles in front of us, but only one at a time. Some of the concerns were questions about the distance from the ocean and the number of sand dunes between the ocean and where our construction would take place. This appeared to be a conservation issue but we had to address it. He next pointed out that the initial permit, for our cottage, called for an 800 gallon septic tank and the current requirement was now 1000 gallons. We had to prove that the initial tank we installed was a 1000 gallon tank, which we knew it was. This required hiring a certified engineering company to examine it and certify its size and location.

The next obstacle was a major one. Our lot was 50' x 100' and Plymouth required a 100' separation between the well and the septic system. When we acquired the initial building permit, they gave us a variance to have a 90' separation. The Board of Health said that the variance no longer applied and they would not approve the permit unless we had a 100' separation. I asked if that was the last objection. He couldn't think of anything else.

I asked if we received permission from the people that owned the lot in front of us to put a well on their property 10' from the property line would that satisfy him. He said as long as they had that right incorporated into the deed it would. Ann and I had always wanted to own the lot between our lot and the ocean, which was classified as an unbuildable lot before we bought our initial property.

Our next step was to track down the owner and see if he would sell us the lot or at least allow a well on it. We found out that the lot was owned by someone who lived across the bay from us. His phone was not listed, so we wrote him a letter explaining our situation. A few weeks went by and we heard nothing. One night Ann and I decided to pay him a visit. He was very sociable, but told us he no longer owned the lot we wanted to buy. He gave that lot and the one next to it to his son. His son lived near him right on the bay but was not home that evening. We asked for his phone number but were told he had an unlisted phone and we should write his son a letter similar to the one we had written to him.

The process started over again, the letter was written with no response, so it was then followed by a visit one evening to the son's home. He didn't want to sell the lot, but he and his wife had started to remodel the kitchen and that was costing them much more than expected. After a few weeks of negotiation we ended up buying the lot in October 1993. This was a major accomplishment. On a worst case condition we at least owned the lot between our cottage and the beach and therefore no matter what happened no one could stop us from having direct access to the beach.

The next task was to establish a well on the new lot 100′ from the existing septic system. Establishing a new well on Saquish was a manual task. It took a day's hard work by hand, using a manual well driver, to drive a stainless steel point about 15′ into the sandy ground. After establishing the well, a hand pump was used to clear out the sand that was in the well water caused by the installation. This was not an easy project and required using your hand to continuously pump the well for a few hours until the water was clear. A sore shoulder that evening really had an impact on your sleep.

The water was tested for drinkable use. It tested positive for everything except salt and iron where the tests were a little high. We had stopped drinking well water after the blizzard of 1978, when the area containing the initial well filled with salt water. We knew the current problem was correctible with the installation of a water filter if the town required it.

I then met with the head of the Health Department and told him about buying the lot at a substantial price to meet his 100' requirement, then installing a well and having the water tested. When I had mentioned buying the lot for a substantial sum of money to meet his requirement, his facial expression changed, indicating this gave him some concern. His attitude then changed to one of support. However, he asked if I took out a permit for the new well. The discussion then evolved around shallow wells installed at Saquish without permits, and since the well was already there what could be done to certify it.

He said that to obtain his final approval there were two things that had to be done. First I had to get a well company that was certified by Plymouth to approve both the well and water quality. Second the two lots had to be combined and recorded as one lot with the Registry of Deeds. There were three well companies that he suggested. I met the owner of one of them and explained the situation and what was needed to meet the Board of Health's approval.

Two employees from the well company came to Saquish and checked the well installation and approved it. I again met with the owner. Since the water was already tested, he did not require another test. However he required us to install a filter to eliminate the high salt and iron content.

We discussed the whole pump and filter situation. The filters required constant pressure, otherwise they would clog. Since there was no electricity, without starting the generator, quite often the pressure would drop very low. This could mean frequent filter changes. Since we had no intention of drinking the water, I told him that once the filters were installed and the testing requirements were met the filters would be removed.

He then asked, "Why the hell are you going to install filters if you are then going to remove them?" My response was "Because that's what you said was needed to get the O.K." Nothing further was said or done regarding the filters.

He would write a letter to the Board of Health that should satisfy their well requirements. We soon received approval, pending combining the two lots into one. An engineering company was hired to survey the lots and file for a new lot with the Registry of Deeds. The permit was then signed by both the Board of Health and the Conservation Department. With these key departments on board the rest of the permitting process was straightforward. The last major hurdle was the public meeting conducted by the Planning Board. If the Planning Board turned us down for something that was not easily correctable, we planned to file an appeal with the State of Massachusetts.

Ann and I wanted an observation room with as large a view of the ocean as possible. Bev McNair had a cottage with large windows on the second floor. We used that as a starting point and discovered the building code did not allow windows closer than 20" from the floor. Next was designing the room.

Our design was a 24' x 18' observation room. It included six 5' x 5' windows each with a companion 2' x 5' rollout for ventilation.

Two were placed on each side and two were placed in the front between the sliding glass doors. The back wall had two 2' high x 5' wide rollouts. This provided a 360º view. Starting with the front beach, then continuing to Brown's Bank, Plymouth Beach then Western Point. To the back was Clarke's Island, the Back Bay, Powder Point Bridge and the road behind Duxbury Beach that led to The Gurnet. The view was completed on the front left with The Gurnet and Gurnet Light.

We then hired an architect to draw the plans, made some changes that we wanted and then filed the final permit with the Planning Board. In mid-July 1994 the Planning Board meeting was held. Les had made everyone in the process aware of what we were doing and discussed any concerns they had, and asked for their support. A number of our friends from the beach, including the Balakiers, Keegans, Hartwicks and Wojnars were at the meeting to support us. By a majority of one, the Planning Board approved our permit. The rest of the members did not vote against us but just abstained from voting. After the meeting we went to Izacck's Restaurant to celebrate.

We received the signed permit on 7/25/94. It was a time consuming effort, but thankfully after retiring, I had the extensive time available to pursue it. The next step was starting to plan for construction. The Building Department allowed us to put a 7' x 4' patio with railings outside of the sliding glass doors and a 2½' extension from the patio around the front and the two sides. There would be no railing on the extension to interfere with the view, since this was not considered a walkway but rather a sun screen.

In early October Les showed up with his crew composed of Carl, Wes and Jimmy. The first day they tore down the 24' x 18' roof in the front part of the cottage. For the night they covered the opening with plastic to prevent any potential rain from leaking into the kitchen and den area. The second day they brought a beam that was 5½" x 14" x 20' long. This beam was the main carrying beam across the center of the cottage. It was made under pressure with wooden strips and glue and was stronger than a steel I beam. It was so heavy that it took five of us to lift it and set the beam in place.

BUILDING THE OBSERVATION ROOM

As work progressed Ann and I slept in the cottage, but quite often used Sandy and Danny's place for lunch since work was going on right above the kitchen. Each day Ann baked a coffee cake or muffins for the working crew to have during their coffee break. They said it was the best they were ever treated on any of their projects.

One day near the end of construction the windows were all installed but there was an open ledge above them. When Ann and I awoke that morning we heard some random banging in the new upstairs room. We thought the workers had arrived early and had used the ladder to access the room through the sliding glass doors as they often did. The banging continued and increased. You could tell it was not a hammer. We wondered what was going on and rushed upstairs to find out. A flock of Barn Swallows, on their fall migration, had landed to rest on the ledge which was right above the windows and was not yet closed in. When they decided to leave, eight of them mistakenly flew into the room. They tried to escape by flying through the windows but all they did was bounce off and land on the floor and then fly up and try again. There was blood and defecation all over the windows and floor. We used a snow shovel to scoop them up and throw them outside through the sliding glass doors. All of them were able to fly away, however a number must have experienced severe headaches when they stopped for the night, on their migration.

During the construction period, which lasted until late October, the weather was perfect without a single day of rain. Les brought the Plymouth inspectors to Saquish and they gave us an occupancy permit. On October 28th, Ann's sister Dot brought my father to the cottage to see the addition and we celebrated his 84th birthday. There is still a sign behind the Knotty Pine finished wall that says, "Happy 84th Birthday Dad." It was 23 years since we built the cottage and Dad had enjoyed every one of them.

During the 23 years Dad and I spent considerable time together fishing, lobstering and clamming. His birthday celebration turned out to be Dad's last visit to Saquish. Five months later he passed away. With his passing, I lost one of my two best friends. He was second only to my wife Ann. From the time I can remember, whenever Dad went fishing or hunting he always took me with him.

I was born a couple of years before World War II started. Shortly after it began, Dad was conscripted by the U.S. Government to work under their control as a private citizen. His specialty was plumbing. His first assignment was at the submarine base in New London, Connecticut. From there he was transferred along with twenty-thousand other construction people to a major government facility in Oak Ridge, Tennessee. One day they were told by the Commanding Officer that if the project they were working on was successful, it would help to bring the war to a quick, successful close. A couple of years later he was transferred to Camp Edwards on Cape Cod. This was just as I started the first grade. For the next two Summers he rented a cottage in Onset, which was just before the bridges that led to the Cape and was very close to the ocean. My mother, sister Barbara and I joined him for the Summers.

Before the two Summers at Onset, I hardly knew my Dad, since he was always away working for the Government. While at Onset that changed. We spent many evenings and weekends together. On an outgoing tide, we would often walk in the marshes between the eel grass and the open bay and catch Blue-shell Crabs as they tried to scramble from the eel grass to the open ocean. You walked very slow and were quiet so they didn't scramble before you had a chance to catch them. Dad made two contraptions, each with a long pole attached to a metal hoop that was fitted with chicken wire. This looked like a long fishing net. It was very effective in catching the crabs as they tried to escape across the shallow water. We also had an inflated tire tube that held a bushel basket which fitted into it. This was easy to pull as it slid on top of the water and could hold a large number of crabs. Just like lobsters, the Blue-shell Crabs are a delicacy.

On weekdays while Dad was working, I with some of my local friends, would go to the beach and play for hours. During these times, I fell in love with the ocean-beach and dreamed about someday owning a cottage on a beach. If you dream long enough and make a commitment to follow through when an opportunity arises, sometimes your dream comes true.

On weekends Dad would take me to an undeveloped area in Plymouth, West of the Cape Cod Canal. You would drive on a number of narrow, gravel roads that crisscrossed and intersected until you came to a large shallow pond. It had old tree trunks sticking out all over the water surface. It was appropriately called "Stumpies." You never saw anyone else there. Dad would use a telescope rod, wade out beyond the weeds and into the stumps. For bait, slices cut from a Yellow Perch's belly was used and skidded across the top of the water just like a small fish trying to escape. Large pickerel, sometimes very large pickerel, would smash the water and murder the bait. Dad caught a large number of pickerel between 20″ and 28″. I wasn't old or big enough to fish the way Dad did so I would stand on the bank, watch and feel very proud each time he caught a large one.

There was a small pond on the opposite side of the gravel road from Stumpies. It had many frogs in it and Dad taught me how to jig frogs. Quite often when fishing was slow, I would go and jig for frogs. Dad would then clean them but as time went on I quickly learned how to do it. For years, until Ann and I were married, we would go harvesting frogs together. Frog legs are still my favorite meal.

The first time I brought Ann home to meet my parents and have dinner, we ate frog legs. When we sat down to eat, Ann looked at her plate and asked Dad what it was that we were going to eat. Dad was not completely honest with Ann because he told her to try it and it would taste very much like chicken. I loved Ann then, I love her now and I will always love her, no matter what she thinks about eating frog legs. She has never prepared them for us!

A few times in the early evening, Dad and I would go to Stumpies and fish for horned pout. They usually bite best after it gets dark and are the best tasting of all fresh water fish. Twice Dad took me to the Cape Cod Canal at night to fish for striped bass. We were novices and had no luck, but these were times I always remembered. During these two Summers I really became close to Dad. Soon after, the war ended and Dad was able to come back home and live with us.

He enjoyed hunting for both pheasants and rabbits. Every Saturday he and his brother Steve would hunt for the whole day. He initially let me join them for part of the day, walk behind them, and learn the rules of hunting and gun safety. The part day then became a full day and I moved from walking behind them to walking in a straight line between them, doubling the amount of territory that we covered. Dad bought me a shot gun and taught me how to use it at a professional shooting range. At age fifteen I acquired a hunting license and already was a well trained hunter, but only lacked actual hunting experience.

During this time Dad also taught me how to fish small brooks for Brook Trout and how to fly cast for trout in streams, ponds and lakes. At age sixteen I joined the Singletary Rod and Gun Club of which Dad was a member. They had a private trout pond which they stocked, and raised Pheasants which they released during the hunting season.

When deer hunting we would jointly stalk them for hours at a time. Never saying a word to each other, but always keeping the florescent color of the other persons clothing in sight. Using only hand signals, you could tell the other person not only what you were going to do, but also what you wanted him to do. This worked as well as talking, sometimes even better. You could easily misinterpret words or sentences, but hand signals, when you have used them with someone for a long time, are very clear. If you talked while stalking deer, you would never see one. Their ability to smell and hear is unbelievable.

As time went on, our hunting and fishing activities continued. When we partnered in building the cottage at Saquish, our time together increased. The amount of time we spent fishing increased substantially, but the days spent hunting decreased. Springs, Summers, and early Falls were all spent at the beach.

During his last few years, Dad's time spent at Saquish had decreased. He had heard much about the observation room we were building and finally had the chance to see it on his 84th birthday. That day the stripers started to break water in front of the cottage and the sea gulls were diving to catch the bait fish that were pushed to the surface. I and some of my friends grabbed our fishing rods and rushed down to the beach to catch the stripers. Dad watched from the windows and this even made his day more enjoyable. It brought back fond memories of when he was able to join us and do this.

After this last visit Ann and I left Saquish to head for Florida for our second season there. The next Summer Les and his workers came back and finished the interior walls with Knotty Pine boards. At this time there was one last project to do. That was to rename the cottage the "IMPOSSIBLE DREAM" and have Bobby Gosselin make a professional sign with that name engraved. We placed it above the inside entrance of our front door.

From that time on, most of our indoor time was spent in the observation room. We had close to a 360 degree view of the ocean that was spectacular. During an extremely high full moon tide, you could sit there and see the ocean water creeping in and then sliding out, climbing and then receding over 14 vertical feet. Ann cooked the meals down stairs and we ate them at the table upstairs. You could watch the sun and moon rise, first peeking then climbing out of the ocean. The couch was a pullout that turned into a bed. This was ideal for our visiting friends who wanted to awake early, watch the sunrise and take an invigorating walk on the beach. Ann and I spent many hours in the lounge chair reading and enjoying the brightness that flowed in from all the large windows.

There is a replica of the Mayflower that is docked in Plymouth Harbor. For an entrance, fee you can tour it and get a feel for what it was like to live on the ship and sail across the Atlantic Ocean in the early sixteen-hundreds. One day each Summer the ship is brought out of the harbor, sailed into the bay and turned around right in front of our cottage. It is then returned to its dock in Plymouth. On a bright sunny day, when you watch this event from our observation room, the view is unbelievable.

Ann and I had fulfilled our IMPOSSIBLE DREAM of a second floor observation room and all the pleasures that went with it.

THE IMPOSSIBLE DREAM

CHAPTER 8

ADDITIONS, ENHANCEMENTS AND RENOVATIONS

ADDITIONS

While we were finishing the interior, Ann was in the process of collecting furniture for the cottage. Some was given to us, and other pieces were bought at yard sales which she went to on Saturday mornings. One day she found a great deal in Duxbury and bought a number of oak antique bureaus for $5 a piece. The tailgate on the Yellowbird was lowered and a couple of antique bureaus were tied down and extended over the tailgate. The bumpy trip back to the beach caused the tailgate and bureaus to bounce up and down. By the time she reached the cottage, the steel connectors that held the end of the tailgate to the vehicle had ripped loose. Ann's antique bargain turned into an expensive tailgate repair.

When we sold our Westboro home in 1994, we stored a number of items in Bev McNair's home in Duxbury. During that time Coco and Terry Gilbert, our new Florida friends, came to visit us. Coco was doing consulting work in Hartford, CT. They flew there, then rented a car and drove to Westboro. Less than a mile from our home, the car broke down. A couple of hours later a replacement car and tow truck arrived from Boston.

The next day Terry and I loaded a kitchen table, four chairs, my antique desk and its companion chair on to my 4-wheel drive pickup truck, which I had just bought after retiring. We then drove to Bev's house with Ann and Coco following in the Jeep Cherokee. The furniture was stored in Bev's cellar where it stayed until we finished our observation room in 1995. The next few days were spent fishing, lobstering, relaxing and enjoying the beach.

During the blizzard of '78 the telephone lines and poles that connected the Coast Guard station on The Gurnet with the mainland were knocked down. We were able to acquire some of the poles that were on Duxbury Beach.

They were used to replace the initial clothes line pole we installed a number of years before. Pole #22, my favorite number, was used to anchor the clothesline to the porch.

Before selling our Westboro home, a large amount of loam was transferred from there to Saquish. The loom was used to build a garden near the hand pump and was enclosed with fencing to keep the rabbits out. In the Spring, when the weather was warm enough, the garden was planted. Radishes grew very rapidly but most of the vegetables did not ripen until early Fall. By that time we had left for Florida. The return was not worth the effort it took, so the garden was turned over to our neighbors Sandy and Dan who still use it. I always ate many radishes before we left.

In the late eighties we were running out of storage space, so a 6' x 8' shed was built in back of the cottage. The shed proved very useful when we decided to install a solar energy system. The roof was used to host the solar panels and a box was built inside the shed to store the ten batteries. For the first time in twenty-five years we had full time electrical power.

Along with solar energy, the coming of cell phones, direct T.V. and high speed, wireless internet connection somewhat modernized life at Saquish.

After the "No Name Storm" of '91, our emergency connection to the outside world was eliminated. The Coast Guard personnel stationed at Gurnet Point were replaced with a wireless connection from Scituate. It controlled Gurnet Light and the foghorn. With the coming of the Ground Positioning System the foghorn was finally eliminated. The cell phones had replaced the CB systems that many of us had and we often used to communicate with each other in addition to the Duxbury and Plymouth Harbor Masters, just like the truckers used them to communicate amongst themselves on the highways.

ENHANCEMENTS

Ann loved flowers but supposedly on beach sand which surrounded the cottage only beach roses grew. She and my mother bought the first rose bush and planted it near the hand pump. There were two types of rose bushes, those with pink blossoms and those with white. We bought a number of both types and planted them. After a couple years Ann discovered she could cut off the shoots, replant them and create her own nursery. This was an ongoing process and a large number of pink and white rose bushes grow in front and on the side of the cottage.

One day Jack Ruprecht, a major land owner on the beach, brought Ann a Yucca plant. He owned a nursery in Kingston, and told her that Yucca plants grow very well in beach sand. She planted it in front of the cottage and the following year the Yucca plant grew a three-foot stock.

A number of white blossoms grow on top of the stock. It is a beautiful plant and the blossoms occur in early July and last two weeks. Ann fell in love with it. After visiting us on the beach, Judy Hall and Elaine Gallo gave Ann a second Yucca plant.

After the plants blossomed, baby Yuccas grow near the roots. These were broken off and replanted. There are over seventy Yucca plants in our sandy area and every year during the first two weeks in July the whole area is covered with elegant white blossoms. A number of Yuccas have been given to friends, either as a gift or in remembrance of a loved one.

She continued to enhance the area around the cottage with flowers and flowering bushes. These include a Scotch Broom, Bay Berry bushes from Lorri and Brian's Nantucket home, Montague Daisies and a Butterfly bush. Some grew in the beach sand and for those that didn't a perennial rock garden with loam was created.

Five wooden barrels of flowers were interspersed around the front yard and four containers of petunias were on the front porch. Each of these were replenished every year.

On one of our trips to Provincetown, with the Balakiers, we bought a swing and a large fish net. The swing was attached to one of the roof trusses in our den and then was moved to one of the roof timbers in the observation room, once that was built. It was initially a big hit with the girls. A number of years later, Ann was able to acquire a dolphin seat which could be interchanged with the adult cushion seat. Cory, Sydney, Michael, Max and other visiting children loved to swing in the dolphin seat. Once the swing was in the observation room, the view overlooking the Front Bay, Gurnet Point and the Lighthouse was overwhelming.

The fish net, which spread-over 20 square feet, was placed on the wall in the downstairs den. It was used to attach items collected from the sea. Many of the items came from Saquish. The rest came from our trips to Florida and the islands in the Caribbean.

The items on the net included the shells of lobsters that had molted in the lobster pots, spider crabs, horse shoe crabs, sand crabs, star fish, fish pouches, sea urchins and many different shells.

A 3½ pound lobster, the biggest we caught that was not a female carrying eggs, was placed on a board covered with plastic and then buried in the sand underneath the cottage. We had taken out the major meat from the tail, but left the remaining lobster intact and not cooked. Two weeks later we uncovered it. The ants had eaten all the meat that was initially left. All that remained was the complete shell, which we varnished and hung on our net.

One day a large commercial fishing boat was anchored in front of the cottage cleaning large sea scallops before going into Plymouth. We took our boat and went to see what was going on. The fishermen threw us some of the large scallop shells. When visiting Milt and Berit Steen in Florida, we went to see if any Blue-shell Crabs were in their crab pot. There were no crabs, just a few small seahorses. We dried the seahorses in the sun. A couple large scallop shells and a few of the dried seahorses were attached to the net.

Our grandchildren also added to our net collection. Cory found a large sand dollar in the Turks and Caicos Islands, Sydney found a horseshoe crab shell near the rocks at Western Point, Michael and Max each found a starfish on the beach. They all placed their items on the net. When they came to Saquish, they all enjoyed standing on the couch in front of the net admiring the treasures that were on it.

Ann's father made towel holders for the bathrooms that were imitations of my lobster buoys. Many compliments were made about them because they were so unusual.

Ann had an oil painting of the original cottage created by Hugh Sloan, a resident of Saquish and a professional artist. It was placed on the back wall of the observation room. This was a surprise Christmas gift that she gave me.

Franz, Kathi's husband, did a charcoal drawing of the two story cottage, that was placed on the guest bedroom wall.

We filled two five-gallon antique water bottles with sea glass. The blue and red pieces, which are the hardest to find, were placed around the edges. This gave them the most visibility. One of the bottles was placed near the steps on the first floor and the second was placed in the observation room.

On a vacation to Aruba, we collected a fair number of very interesting shells. Ann made an oval shell mirror to hang in our main bathroom. With the observation room completed a second mirror was made for the top of the steps.

When Anna Hartwick redid her bathroom in Florida, she gave us a large rectangular mirror that we brought back to Saquish. It became a 4' x 3' shell mirror for the girls' bedroom. For the guest bedroom Ann made a diamond shaped mirror and for ours a shell wreath. She made lighted shell trees for both the observation room and the girl's room.

Of all the shell work Ann did, her masterpiece by far was a large headboard mirror that was placed over the bed in the guest room.

When the observation room was finished, 60' of cornices crowned the large windows and door. Ann wanted to place unique cobalt blue glass pieces on all of them.

There was a large antique mall North of Gainsville, FL. On our trips back and forth, it was a convenient place to stop for a break.

Ann would cover the right side of the mall and I the left. At a set time we would meet at the cashier's location with the cobalt blue pieces we had each picked out. The three or four most unique pieces were bought and each year we would add six to eight pieces to our collection. When we were finished buying, there were over seventy unique cobalt blue glass pieces in the collection.

Hanging from the rafters on the room's east side were six cobalt blue stars, bought at a craft fair in Fort Myers, and a cobalt blue ball from Paula and Dave Carlson. This looked like a miniature solar system display.

On the cornices that were over the two front downstairs windows she had a collection of antique irons. All the downstairs cornices were decorated with shells and painted white to provide a contrast with the Knotty Pine woodwork.

Between the rafters on the east wall were a number of ceramic ducks and birds. The front had a ceramic lighthouse collection. Over the kitchen cabinets were a host of large shells we collected from Florida and the Caribbean Islands.

Along with what we had collected, Ann's brother Ray gave us a beautiful large shell he found when stationed in Okinawa. My grandmother also gave us two unique pieces of coral that she had for a long time.

Ann is an excellent designer of both the interior house and exterior landscaping. Her design work was just a small part of the contribution she made during the forty years we spent at Saquish. Ann was the heart and soul of the whole operation. She not only enhanced the good times, but willingly stepped in to help during the tough times. Right from the start she prepared the weekend meals for Dad and me when we went to the beach to work. This was easier for us and much more delicious than the few sandwiches Dad and I would have prepaid if we had to do it ourselves. It also gave us the strength to continue working on the construction project. During the finishing of construction, the steaks and extra goodies she packed were delicious. Even our dog Jake enjoyed the steaks, sometimes without permission.

When the construction was under way, along with taking care of the girls, Ann stained the sub-flooring in the garage and shopped for all the odds and ends we would need during the weekends. In June when all the girls came to the beach on Sundays, Ann stained the 4' X 8' Texture 111 sheets on saw horses behind the cottage. During this time of extensive work, she would praise Dad and me and give us encouragement. This boosted our moral and helped make the evening and weekend work a challenge and not a burden. Her work and support were very instrumental in helping us to meet our personal commitment of finishing the exterior building by the 4th of July 1971.

Ann and I equally enjoyed the years at Saquish. There were many events and activities that we enjoyed together and many that we enjoyed individually. These were the results of hard work on both our parts, but it didn't stop there.

The time and effort she spent in assisting me in writing and editing this book was substantial. If I had to measure the difference over the 40 years, she worked much harder than I did.

RENOVATIONS

Shortly after the observation room was completed, the foundation planks and floor joists on the outside rows of the foundation started to decay. Since they were not pressurized, the rain and moisture from the ocean weather had an impact on them. The center row of railroad ties, which were not exposed were still intact. I hired a local contractor who had done work near the ocean. He and his partner delivered one hundred 16' long pressurized planks to the beach and unloaded them in back of the cottage. The contract called for them to replace the foundation planks and then Ann and I would install the new floor joists. On one side at a time, they used construction jacks to lift the floor joists off the foundation. They then removed the double row of 2" x 12" x 16' planks which were decayed. Since the new planks were not full size, they used triple planks on each side for the foundation and nailed the floor joists back to the foundation planks.

For the next year Ann and I installed the new floor joists. Since the plywood floor was nailed to the original joists we had to place the new joists up against the old joists. We then nail them together before nailing the new floor joists to the new foundation planks. This was much harder than it first appeared.

You could not slide the new joist in because it bound up against the foundation and the sub-floor. The joist was slipped in at an angle with the top against the sub-floor. The bottom of the joist was then placed against the foundation planks about three to six inches away from the old joist. Two screw down clamps were used, one next to each of the foundation rows to pull the new joist up against the old joist. Quite often the clamps were not strong enough to pull the joists together and they would bind.

A sledgehammer was then used to pound the new joist alternately near each side of the foundation rows. You first banged the joist near the outside row, then crawled underneath the cottage, and then banged it near the inside row. After each hit the clamp was reinstalled and tightened to stop the joist from springing loose. This process of moving and banging, from outside to inside, was repeated until the new joist snapped into place. Then it was nailed to the old joist and foundation. When we reached the shed, the top of it was ripped out to get the joists in, and then it was reassembled. Ann and I worked better as a team than we ever had. There was no way I could have competed this project by myself.

A couple of years later, after the winter winds had blown away some sand from under the cottage, I discovered that the telephone poles carrying the outside foundation rows had decayed a couple of inches below the sand. With all the rain over the years, the water had drained into the sand and pocketed around the poles. It took a long time to dry, thus softening and decaying the poles. They had to be replaced. Another major two-person project. When building the cottage, installing the carrying poles was one of the hardest projects we had. To dig them out and replace them would be even harder.

Ethan Balakier was home from college for the Summer. He worked with me on this project. Sixteen poles had to be replaced with 8" x 8" pressurized timbers of various lengths, up to 16' long. I bought them from Taylor Lumber in Marshfield, made four trips with my pickup truck and brought them to Saquish.

To remove the old poles we had to lift the new foundation beams then remove and replace the poles one at a time. We used four large manual construction jacks and two heavy planks. One set was used on each side of the pole. The jacks were slowly turned one at a time. Once the weight of the foundation was lifted off the pole, the 10" galvanized bolt that connected the foundation to the pole was removed. The next step was to dig an angled trench from the outside of the foundation to the bottom of the pole. The sand around the pole was removed and a sledgehammer was used to knock the pole out from under the foundation and into the trench. The antique ice tongs again proved invaluable in dragging the old poles up and out of the trench and to maneuver the new heavy timbers.

Once an old pole was removed, we cut a new timber to an exact duplicate of the one removed, including the notch that would hold up the foundation. This time however, the use of the electric generator, a skill saw, a Saws-all and a high powered electric drill made this part of the job much easier.

The new timber was slipped down the trench until it was in the right position and then was flipped up and under the foundation. The timber was attached to the foundation with a new 10" galvanized bolt and we moved on to the next pole. We used wooden shims so that everything was tight.

The project was started with the back poles, initially where the sand was only five feet deep. Things went well until we reached the front of the cottage where the sand was over ten feet deep. In addition the weather for the week was extremely hot and humid, but we continued. At the six-foot level and beyond, we had to make potential escape steps in the trench. At this point we were unable to easily shovel the sand up and out.

One of us would then stand on the porch with a rope tied to a five-gallon bucket and lower it over the porch rail. The other would fill the bucket with sand. It was then pulled up, emptied out and lowered back down again to repeat the process. Along with handling the bucket, the person on the porch had to watch for the trench to potentially start collapsing, which happened a number of times. Once below the six foot level, it was possible to be buried alive. Before the trench collapsed you could see a crack appear in the sand near the edge of the trench and it would slowly start to expand. A quick yell and the person in the trench would turn and start up the steps as fast as he could. We always made it to safety, but at times were buried from the waist down. Next we had to dig ourselves out, widen the trench and dig out the collapsed sand.

During this time of intense heat, Ann would bring us glasses of ice water and cold towels. We would wrap the towels around our heads, neck and shoulders. This would help to cool us down and refresh us. It made us feel good. She also encouraged us to stop working, almost demanding that we stop, but to no avail.

After this project, all other replacement activity was simple. Every 2" x 8" floorboard on the porch and every 4" x 4" post that carried the porch rails was changed to pressurized wood. We also replaced one of our old gas refrigerators with a new one that had a larger freezer.

Once the solar system was installed, all the gaslights were converted to electric lights. Since the gas pipes that connected the lights to the gas cylinders had rusted, eleven of the gas lights were removed. However, to preserve twenty-five years of nostalgia, one that was attached to the den wall was left. Propane was still used for the refrigerators, stove, hot water heater and generator. The main gas line was made of cast iron and after thirty plus years had started to rust. I arranged to have it replaced with new fiberglass gas pipe, but the person that I hired never showed up. Danny Keegan hired someone he knew from his construction job and one evening he and Danny installed the new fiberglass gas pipe line. We no longer had any worries about potential gas leaks. Our second hand Onan Generator had been with us for over thirty years and was now giving us problems.

Brian Ryder, Lorri's husband was able to get us a new Honda Generator. He and Richard Bien whose work dealt with gas generators, installed the new Honda. Danny installed the cast iron pipe from the generator to the new propane bottles that we placed on the outside of the shed. The generator coupled with the fiberglass pipes gave us a brand new propane system.

One last major project was putting vinyl siding on all sides of the cottage. This eliminated the need to stain the cottage every couple of years. For this project all Ann and I did was to hire a company to do the work.

We just sat back and enjoyed watching the project from start to finish. It was a pleasure to think about the free time we would have in no longer staining the cottage.

Every year there were minor replacement and renovations required. I have touched on those that were the most interesting, had the most effect and required the most effort. There was no end to the work involved in maintaining a summer cottage on the ocean. However, it went with the territory. At times it was irritating and at other times rather enjoyable.

Anytime we needed help there were a number of people at Saquish with various skills and abilities that would give you a hand. Two people that were always there, often anticipating when help was needed, were my two closest neighbors, Danny Keegan and Richard Balakier. They joined right in and to both of them I am deeply grateful.

CHAPTER 9

SHELLFISH

Shellfish are often referred to as clams, and gathering shellfish is often referred to as clamming.

For the first thirty years clams, lobsters and fish were plentiful. They composed most of our protein diet during the summer months. As time went on, the available stock of these creatures decreased, mainly due to over harvesting. Some specific types of clams and fish have started to make a comeback, but none are near the numbers they were in the seventies.

When you went clamming in the Saquish area, there were five different types of shellfish you could gather. They are razor clams, sea clams, quahogs, soft shell clams and muscles.

The primary condition for shell fishing was a low tide. The lower the tide the more accessible the shellfish. Initially, licenses were required, but there was little enforcement. As time went on and stocks were depleted and enforcement increased. Around the turn of the century most clamming was legally stopped in Plymouth, but a short clamming season has recently opened. You could always buy a Duxbury license and clam near The Gurnet Road.

The first clamming we did was for razor clams, on the sand bars near The Gurnet. They were used for flounder and cod fishing and were excellent bait. They were also available in the Back Bay, but in smaller quantities. Now there are a fair number of razors found on the sandbars and mudflats off The Gurnet Road.

Once Ann tried to prepare razors for us to eat, and was told how to deep-fry them. They were washed, dried with paper towels then dipped in flour, eggs and bread crumbs. Not realizing that the razors still maintained a fair amount of water, after preparing them, she dropped them into a fryer. Once they hit the hot oil they exploded. Little balls of burning oil flew out of the pot and hit Ann's face. We rushed Ann into the shower, turned on the cold water and held her while she shivered unmercifully. This however decreased the severity of the burns. We didn't eat razor clams that evening and never attempted to eat them again!

Sea clams are much bigger than any of the other clams. After a very low tide you walk onto the drying sandbars off The Gurnet and on Brown's Bank and look for spots of water that a sea clam has spit up. Then with a clamming rake you dig them out of the sand. They are good for clam patties and chowder. Some fishermen also use a whole sea clam for bait when fishing for stripers and are quite successful.

Initially, we quahoged in the mudflats on the Duxbury Bay side of Saquish. You wore old sneakers laced as tight as you could. A small pole, used as a balancing staff was carried in one hand while the other pulled a plastic sled with a large bucket on it.

You would slosh through the mud, often sinking in it up to your ankles. Mud that was two to three inches deep was ideal for quahogs. You would keep sloshing around until a quahog was felt under one of your feet. Once a quahog was found there often were a number of additional ones nearby.

The old sneakers were used to prevent cuts or gashes from broken glass or old rusty metal that was lodged in the mud. The staff was used for balance while the quahog was retrieved and put in the basket or if your feet became stuck in the mud and you were about to fall. Then you would put your weight on the staff while extracting one foot at a time and would carefully take small steps forward or backward until you reached more solid ground.

One weekend Charlie and Sue Judge, our Westboro next door neighbors were visiting us. There was a very low tide so we went quahoging. They each were given a staff and explained its purpose for balancing and extracting yourself from the mud.

After we were sloshing around in the flats for a while we heard a "flop." There was Charlie laying flat on his back. He had tried to extract himself by leaning backwards and not putting all of his weight on the staff. When getting up he tried to move forward, but again did not put all his weight on the staff, and fell flat on his face. Charlie repeated the whole process one more time, fell back then forward. Then he was able to stabilize himself, slowly extracting one foot, taking a step forward, and then extracting the other. He finally learned how to do it, unfortunately a little too late. Charlie looked like a mud wrestler who had wrestled with a bear. Sue, Ann and I held on to our staffs, but nearly fell down from laughing so hard. We then sloshed our way back to the car, pulling our sled with the quahog baskets behind us. No quahogs Charlie! This scenario was relived a number of times when the four of us would get together, always generating some good laughs, and reliving that weekend.

There was a time when we were harvesting quahogs and a heavy fog rolled into the flats. It didn't take long before we lost all sense of direction.

Every time the foghorn sounded, the location of the source seemed to come from a different place. After that we always had a compass with us whenever we went for quahogs, striped bass or cod. There were a number of times when the compass came in handy when we were caught in the fog, since you always knew the general direction back to the peninsula.

You could rake for quahogs on the Duxbury sandbar and mud flats during any low tide. We finally bought a Duxbury license and then only went quahoging there. Quahogs had to be two inches long and you were often checked by wardens. A round ring with a two inch diameter was used to measure them. If the quahog fell through, it was too small. While raking for quahogs, sea clams were also found. Razor clams were common on the sandbar and mud flats. Kosher salt was sprinkled in each razor clam hole that we found. After a few minutes a number of razor clams would pop up out of the ground and were just picked up. How easy!

The small quahogs were called little necks. They are sold in many supermarkets. Topped with horseradish, cocktail sauce and a little Tabasco sauce they are eaten raw as an appetizer, often with saltines. Many restaurants, especially Italian ones, also serve them as linguine with white clam sauce. The bigger quahogs were ground up with Ritz crackers, garlic, onions, celery and Old Bay Seasoning. The stuffing was placed back into a clean quahog shell and baked in an oven. This resulted in baked stuffed quahogs which were excellent. They were also used in chowder.

The same flats that were good for quahogs, were also good for soft shell clams. While gathering them you knelt down and used a clam rake to dig into the sand and then turn it over. You were careful not to break or crack the soft shells. This was not easy to do. The clams that were cracked or broken were used to make clam cakes or for bait when flounder and cod fishing. In a good clamming location, you could gather a decent number of these clams in a 3' x 3' area. The clams existed all the way from the creek at The Gurnet to the cove at the north side of Western Point.

As you entered Saquish Beach, the rocks and sea grass on the left also had some soft shell clams but it was hard digging in the rocky soil. They didn't last long in this area and soon disappeared. When clamming was prohibited by Plymouth, soft shell clams were available in Duxbury Bay. Digging in the eel grass was illegal, as it was in Plymouth, so you had to dig in the sand that was just before the grass.

When I went soft shell clamming at Western Point, Ann would often come with me and picked mussels that were attached to the rocks near Bennet's Point. On a very low tide she accompanied me to the Duxbury flats and harvested mussels that were attached to rocks way out in the bay.

There were commercial fishermen who gathered boatloads of mussels from beds that were just North of Clark's Island.

We initially did not eat mussels until one day when we decided to try them. They were steamed with sliced onions, garlic, celery, wine and Old Bay Seasoning. We were converted after the first meal. This is Ann's favorite shellfish. Mine is soft shell clams, dunked in melted butter and eaten with saltines.

For years the clamming was so good that you could fill most of a five gallon bucket in nothing flat. The commercial clammers would haul out bushels of soft shell clams at a time and, from Duxbury Bay, it was boatloads of mussels at a time. Unfortunately, all good times often come to an end.

Every now and then you would find a scallop with no idea from where it originated. There were no scallop beds anywhere nearby. Recently commercial oystering has flourished in Duxbury with companies given specific areas to use. Some oysters with shell figurations that make them unmarketable are released in another part of the bay and are gathered by people who have clamming licenses. One of the Duxbury companies now distributes top notch oysters to many places in the world.

Plymouth has recently issued permits to start oyster farms in the waters within its jurisdiction, and a few Saquish people have acquired them. A new and hopefully profitable adventure, for those with the fortitude to attempt it.

CHAPTER 10

COD, FLOUNDER, & OTHER FISH

One of the necessities for ocean activities was owning a boat. During my time at Saquish we owned five different boats. The first was an 18' Penn Yan that we bought with a trailer. The trailer was modified and proved extremely valuable in hauling building materials. The boat was never used. It was brought to the beach, stored behind the cottage and then sold. It was impractical to use while lobstering and not necessary for fishing the bays, when compared to a smaller aluminum boat. Even though we started with a twelve foot aluminum boat pulled by a make shift skid, we needed a boat that we could leave on a trailer and park in front of the cottage.

When used, the trailer was attached to the trailer hitch on the SUV, then driven down to the water. The trailer was backed into the water and the boat pushed off. This was similar to launching a boat from a boat ramp. After returning from lobstering or fishing, the whole procedure was done in reverse. A winch was used to lift the boat from the water and pull it onto the trailer. It had to be a boat that was light enough for one person to handle. A fourteen foot long aluminum boat met this need, and this is what we used for the rest of our time at Saquish.

If the surf was rough and the wind was blowing, launching and lifting the boat from the water proved to be quite an effort. Every now and then, on a very windy day, the hitch from the winch was attached to the front of the boat and the boat was dragged out of the water on to the dry beach. From there the winch was used to pull the boat onto the trailer. This eliminated any interference from the wind in trying to lift the boat onto the trailer while the trailer was in the water.

On returning from lobstering or fishing, there would be seaweed or other messy items scattered on the bottom of the boat. Once the boat was back on the trailer, the drain plug was removed and buckets of sea water were poured into the boat. Everything that didn't belong would pour out the drain. The boat and trailer were then returned and parked near the sand dune in front of the cottage, clean and ready for the next lobstering or fishing trip.

During the initial stages of construction, we bought a twelve foot aluminum boat with a twelve horse power motor. This served our need for a few years, but as we kept wandering further out in the ocean to fish for cod and to chase after schools of striped bass in the bays, we needed a bigger boat with a faster motor. A 14' aluminum boat and a twenty five to thirty horse power motor fit the bill. During the rest of our time at Saquish we bought three boat and motor combinations of this type. They all proved very effective, but the initial two were destroyed by storms. With this in mind, let's move on to their use in fishing and lobstering activities.

Cod and flounder were very abundant in the seventies and eighties. The coming of new and improved technology such as depth finders, fish finders, ground positioning systems and enhanced draggers helped to devastate the cod and flounder stocks. Even though some of these technologies helped the recreational fisherman, they also greatly enhanced the commercial fishing industry.

The commercial dominance of the management fishing councils, which set the fishing rules and regulations, played to the commercial interests. In fairness to them their interest focused mainly on the short-term revenue potential, this year's income, and not necessarily on the long term health of the industry.

During this time cod were easy to catch. The basic fishing grounds were two to eight miles off The Gurnet and one could catch enough cod for a few meals on a random three-hour excursion. Cod liked rocky ocean bottoms with a quick drop off of two or more feet. This was the same type of ocean bottom that lobsters liked. Therefore the best cod grounds were easily defined by strings of commercial lobster pots. A string consisted of ten pots connected by a strong rope line with a buoy visible at each end of the line.

Every now and then, on a calm sunny day we would venture out half way to Provincetown and fish in water 100' deep. Our eyes would always keep checking the east and north horizons watching for large black clouds that might appear. When this happened, a major thunder storm that could change a calm, sunny day into torrential rains with gusts of winds of up to thirty miles an hour, could be less than one half hour away.

When we saw these clouds appear, we would start our motor and hightail it back toward shore, trying to cover as much distance as possible while the ocean was still calm. Sometimes it would be a false alarm. Other times, with one exception, we always made it back before the storm hit. On the one exception, we were one half mile from shore when the clouds broke open. Since we had rounded The Gurnet we were protected from the driving winds and only were soaked by the heavy down pour.

When cod fishing, lead jigs or a cod rig made with two hooks, baited with clams and connected to a heavy sinker caught the most cod. When there was little or no wind, letting the boat drift with the tide through the lobster pots produced the most fish. When your hook or jig caught a rope connecting two pots, you often had to break the line. The pots were at a depth of sixty feet or more and there was no way to lift them up to the boat to unhook your cod rig. If a cod was caught on a drift you would repeat the drift until none were caught on two or three separate drifts.

If it was windy, the boat would move too fast to keep the bait on the bottom, so either an anchor was used or a five gallon bucket filled with water was attached to the back of the boat to slow it down. If nothing was caught in a short time, either the anchor location was changed or a different pot location was tried. As time went on increasingly more Sand Sharks congregated off The Gurnet and became a pain in the ass. They would bite before the bait hit the bottom, and their slashing sharp tails were dangerous when unhooking them.

In the Fall, schools of cod would run into Duxbury Bay. During the outgoing tide, if you anchored at the #4 buoy near Clark's Island or in the main channel near The Gurnet, cod would continuously bite as they migrated back to the deeper ocean. Often you could hook one, bring it in, unhook it, drop the line back in the water and have another one hooked within a couple of minutes. This would last for approximately half an hour. Then the school was gone. In two weekends we would catch enough cod to stock our freezer and have enough to eat until the following Spring. During the early nineties cod fishing deteriorated and this continued for the next ten to fifteen years. Over the last few years it has slowly started to come back.

Flounder fishing was initially fantastic. The best area was between the two green buoys in front of the cottage. As you started to enter Plymouth, Duxbury and Kingston Harbors, the main channel was to the right of the buoys and Brown's Bank was to the left. You didn't want to end up on the bank, for fear of getting stuck in the sand and being tipped over by the out rushing tide. Therefore you anchored firmly in the channel. Fishing was best from two hours before high tide until two hours after the tide.

A flounder rig consists of a large sinker with a hook on each side. I always used a fishing rod while Ann, Kathi and Lorri used a hand line. Dad always used two hand lines, one over each side of the boat. Once the sinker hit the bottom you pulled the line up about a foot, counted to five then jerked the line up another foot. If there was no fish tugging on the line you would let it sink again and keep repeating the process for about three minutes.

If you didn't have a fish hooked by then, you pulled the line in and checked the bait. If you had a fish on the first or any other pull, you let the line stay there, counted to five and pulled again. About one in ten times you ended up with another fish caught at the same time. It took about one to two hours to fill a five-gallon bucket with good sized flounder. Enough were filleted to eat for the week. The rest were put in a large container, stored in a refrigerator and later used for lobster bait.

One time while Dad, Gene and I were flounder fishing, Dad sat in the front of the boat and Gene in the back. I had quit smoking a couple of years earlier and Gene had just quit. Dad was in the process of quitting, by smoking half a cigarette at a time. Shortly after we started to fish Dad lit up a cigarette, smoked half and threw the remaining half over the side. Gene intensely watched it go by on the outgoing tide.

A short while later the same process happened again and then it was followed for the third time. With this Gene said, "Blank blank Stash, which was the Polish nickname for Stan. I've just stopped smoking and that's the third cigarette butt you've thrown over the side with half the cigarette still good. I almost jumped overboard to get the last one as it went by me." That was the last cigarette that Stash lit until we were back on shore.

In the early nineties flounder fishing, just like cod fishing, slowly deteriorated until the early two thousands when it had all but disappeared. However flounder like cod has started to rejuvenate.

Every year, just before Memorial Day, large schools of mackerel would arrive and stay near the big green buoy that marked the entrance to Plymouth, Kingston and Duxbury Harbors. They would then move out further into Cape Cod Bay and stay for most of the Summer. Schools of large striped bass would follow the mackerel. With the coming of bluefish, the mackerel stayed for a short time and then migrated North to Maine.

A mackerel jig consists of a silver spoon tied to the end of a string of five hooks with different colored plastic tubing on each hook. Once the first mackerel hit the silver spoon, the rest of the school would attack the plastic covered hooks. Six mackerel were often hooked at the same time. Before you landed them in the boat, some would shake off the hooks.

When the water was calm and the mackerel were near the surface, you could tell if a school of them was moving. There was rippling water that existed over the top of the school. When the ripples were coming toward the boat, it was just a matter of time before a number of them were hooked. Then you saw hundreds, if not thousands, of them passing under the boat. After a short time, either the school would circle back or a new school would approach the boat and the fun would start again.

Every now and then when the silver spoon hit the bottom a decent sized cod would engulf the spoon just as the jigging process started. Once when Gene and I were fishing a few miles East of The Gurnet, we saw a school of very large fish breaking up out of the water while feeding on a school of smaller fish. It had to be a school of large Blue Fin Tuna chasing a school of mackerel. The fish were the biggest we had ever seen.

Mackerel are very good lobster bait, second only to bluefish. They also are very good bait for striped bass. They have a stronger taste than we liked and initially we didn't eat them. After discovering how to prepare and cook bluefish, mackerel done the same way and cooked the day they were caught turned out to be very enjoyable.

Tautog (black fish) and fluke were there at various times during the year. Tautog frequented the rocks around The Gurnet and fluke were mainly in the Duxbury Harbor Channel. Fluke tasted like flounder and tautog were the best tasting salt water fish, second only to haddock. Its skin, however, was very tough to cut and remove making cleaning it a chore. We never focused on either one, but every now and then we'd catch one while fishing for either flounder or striped bass. There were times when a tautog would show up in a lobster pot. Many other species were randomly caught when flounder or cod fishing. These included sea perch, skates, scalpin, silver hake, mud hake, blowfish conga eels and pollack.

Sea perch were excellent eating but were rather small and only the very large ones were worth the time to fillet. They were great at stealing your bait while cod fishing.

Skates, one of the members of the ray family, laid their eggs in pouches which were small, black and rectangular in shape. There were small extensions sticking out of the four corners. The pouches would often wash up onto the beach and people would collect them and use them as ornaments. Hake were part of the cod family. The meat of the silver hake was much softer than cod and though edible, we never tired it. The mud hake was brown in color and the meat was totally described by its name, at least in texture. If you were adrift in the ocean for a number of days without food, and you were able to catch one, you might attempt to eat it.

Scalpins were larger than sea perch and had sharp points sticking out of their back and sides. Watch out! When blowfish were lifted into the boat, their bellies would puff up and they would make a small grunting noise. Conga eels were snake like creatures, much thicker than fresh water eels and had large mouths, as big as a Diamondback Rattlesnake, and teeth that looked more vicious. When their slashing tails hit your fishing line, it ended up in many knots.

Then you had to cut the line and let the eel swim away. Every now and then Dad would take one back to the cottage, clean it and have it for dinner.

All the species just described were either released or used for lobster bait. Over the last number of years they have either substantially decreased in numbers or have disappeared from our fishing grounds.

At times schools of small pollack would show up in the bay. You would think they were blues or small stripers breaking the water, until you launched the boat and went out to catch them. What a disappointment! They too have disappeared from the fishing grounds. Although edible they were not as good as cod and too small to make cleaning them worthwhile. Large pollack and haddock although available before we built at Saquish, never frequented the local fishing grounds in the forty years we spent there.

There was another large unique fish that no one caught but every now and then a dead one washed onto the beach. It was called a goose fish and was shaped like a large skate or ray. The mouth was well over one foot long and could open very wide. It would hide amongst the rocks, open its mouth and when a lobster was seeking cover, it would back into the mouth. One day when Ann and the girls were walking the beach, they found a large dead one that had washed up. They dragged it a mile back to the cottage and it was used for lobster bait.

For years tuna fishing was a big item for a number of people at Saquish. The Japanese were buying tuna for sushi and were paying a very good price. They had a business operation at Green Harbor in Marshfield. The tuna grounds were at Stellwagon Bank that was near Provincetown, eighteen miles East of The Gurnet. My next door neighbor Richard Balakier and his friend Tommy Barton were really into this endeavor.

When you caught a tuna, which could weigh upwards to over a thousand pounds, you towed it back to the Japanese operation in Marshfield and a forklift was used to pick it up from the water. Then a chainsaw was used to cut off the head, tail and fins. Next the insides were removed and the body was loaded into a container that was filled with ice and water. The container was then driven to Boston and flown to Japan. In a couple of weeks you would receive a check based on the quality of the fish and the market price on the day it reached Japan. As the demand for sushi increased, so did the price for tuna and the number of people that fished for them. At its peak, the first few tuna caught, early in the season, brought between twenty and thirty dollars a pound.

Kevin Scola was a name well known by all those that fished for tuna. He was considered, by far, the best individual tuna fisherman. Everyone tried to copy him, but no one, I know, found out how he did it.

There also was a religious sect known as the Moonies. They had a Mother Ship which was the home base of their operation. It would anchor in the tuna grounds and had sleeping quarters, dining facilities and stocked fishing bait. A number of smaller boats carrying two members each would leave the Mother Ship and fish a short distance away. When they caught a tuna they would bring it back to the home base, reload with bait and return to fish. If the fishing was good, the Mother Ship would return to port, unload the tuna, restock the bait and return to the fishing grounds. This would allow the members to fish from sunrise to sunset and maximize the catch. They were by far the best tuna fishing organization and caught the most.

The first time I went tuna fishing, it was with Richard and Tommy, both experienced tuna fishermen. During the previous number of years, they had caught a fair amount of tuna. You started before sunrise and brought with you over thirty pounds of various thrash fish that was used for bait to establish a chum line. My friends had a mooring at Stellwagon Bank.

On the bank there was a large number of boats each one close to the other. The rule was that if one boat hooked up with a tuna and the tuna was pulling the boat, it had the right of way. You unhooked your boat from the mooring and moved it out of the way. The first time there, I saw a tuna pull a decent size boat backwards for well over a mile.

The fishing process was to let out five hand lines with balloons tied to the ends. The balloons were spaced so that the depth of the bait was between 20' and 60' deep, ten feet apart. The hand lines were each rolled up in an individual round bushel basket, with a large floatable ball at the end that was placed outside the basket. After all the lines were out, bait was cut into small pieces and pushed off the back of the boat. This coupled with the current would set up a chum line.

If a tuna crossed the chum line, he would follow it back to the source eating each piece until he reached and swallowed the one with the baited hook in it. Then all hell would break loose. One of the balloons would disappear under the water and one of the hand lines would peel out of the basket.

When this happened, we all had specific tasks to perform. Tommy was to pull in the other hand lines. Richard was to unhook the boat from the mooring and then help Tommy. I was to quickly put on a pair of asbestos gloves and grab the peeling line. With my feet against the back of the boat, I was to stop the tuna from gaining a head of steam, if possible. If I did this, we would alternate in holding on to the line, and let the tuna tow the boat backwards until we tired him out. If I couldn't stop him, then the line was released and the large ball was thrown over the side. We would chase the ball with the boat until we seized the line and would start manually retrieving the line and let the tuna continue to tow the boat.

That morning, halfway through setting up, a large tuna, chasing a bluefish broke water fifty feet from the boat. Soon a balloon disappeared and all hell, in fact, did break lose. Line peeled out of the basket and we all executed our assigned duties to perfection. However we soon discovered it was not a tuna, just a 200-pound blue shark and our attitudes quickly changed from high expectations to complete disappointment. This is typical of the highs and lows associated with any type of fishing, especially tuna fishing where the fish could weigh over one thousand pounds and be worth thousands of dollars. Like most fishermen, however we quickly shrugged it off and went on with our endeavor.

At midday a large whale, much bigger than our boat, rolled up out of the water a few feet from us. It was close enough that you could have reached out and touched it. Frightening, very frightening! We did not catch any tuna, but the day was both enjoyable and educational.

Shortly after the movie "Jaws" was released, a number of people were running up and down Saquish beach yelling "Shark, shark, get out of the water." A fish with a large fin sticking up was swimming very close to shore. Even though it had a large fin, its movements were not those of a shark, but rather it was slow and lethargic.

As increasingly more people gathered at the shore, Phil Rawinski, a very knowledgeable and good fisherman, identified it as a sunfish. A sunfish is round just like a large sea turtle but much bigger in diameter. The fin is located right in the center of its back, making it look just like a shark when its swimming near the surface. With the identification, the panic was over and everyone returned to what they were doing, mainly relaxing on the beach.

CHAPTER 11

LOBSTERING

After a storm in March of 1971, at the time we were building the cottage, Dad and I found a few wooden lobster pots that had washed up on the beach and were abandoned. They needed repair. That happened a few more times that Spring. This generated our interest in lobstering and we applied for and received lobster permits.

Wooden pots, also called traps, were the only type available when we started to lobster. When they were first used, they needed a couple of large rocks placed inside them. This would hold them solidly on the ocean bottom. A couple of days later, after the water penetrated the wood and weighed them down, the rocks were removed. The lobster ropes, which connected the pot to the buoy, were presoaked in pails of water. This would allow them to immediately sink and prevented passing motorboats from cutting them. In a couple of days the pots were ready to catch lobsters.

After a couple of months, barnacles and seaweed would attach to the traps and ropes. This made them heavier and harder to pull up and lift into the boat. Then the pots were taken out of the water, brought to shore and strung out in a line above the high tide level. After drying for two days they were scrapped with a wire brush to remove the dried barnacles and seaweed. The initial launching procedure was then repeated. Before lobstering the next year, the traps were repaired. The nets were tightened and their frayed or broken lines were replaced.

The last four digits of your Social Security number was your lobstering I.D. number. It was burnt one-eighth of an inch into both your buoy and wooden trap. Our first question was. "How do you burn your I.D. numbers in your pots and buoys?" Unlike his son, Dad was very good at fixing and making things with his hands. He took two metal coat hangers, and with two pair of pliers, bent the coat hangers into the numbers 0, 2, 8 and 9 which then covered all the different numbers we needed. Each number was connected to a ten inch piece of coat hanger bent at a ninety degree angle. This ten inch piece is what we held. The number was then heated with a blow torch and then pressed into the wooden pot and buoy. The wood was hard so you had to heat the number a couple of times to get the correct depth.

The buoy was made of styrofoam so a slight touch was all that was needed. After wire pots became available, we still used the coat hanger numbers for our buoys.

I selected yellow and blue as my colors which were also recorded on your license. Dad used the same colors, but we painted our buoys in a different design so we could tell them apart. In the eighties wire traps were produced. They were much lighter and did not require anything to weigh them down. You simply went to a marine store, bought a plastic card and had your I.D. stamped in it.

The design of the trap was interesting. It was split into two distinct areas. The front part had two net entrances, one on each side, where the lobster could enter. The bait was suspended from a metal hook and hung between the two entrances. This area was called the kitchen. A net was attached in the middle to the top, bottom and both sides of the trap. It then tapered toward the back. Where the net came together it was connected by two lines to the back corners of the pot half way between the top and bottom. The back area was called the parlor.

Once a lobster had entered the kitchen it would back up on the inclined net, sit on its tail and feed on the bait. Since a lobster moved backwards, once it had finished eating it would back further up the incline and then fall through the tapered net into the parlor. In the parlor there were two escape vents that allowed undersized lobsters to go free, if they wanted to or found out how to do it. Many, however for whatever reason, remained in the trap.

The keepable lobsters were pegged or banded to stop them from biting other lobsters or people when handled and stored in a keeper pot, which was called a lobster pound. First wooden pegs followed by plastic pegs were used. Then strong rubber bands with a tool to expand and slip them over the claws became available. This replaced the wooden and plastic pegs.

A lobster has the power to crush a finger if its crusher claw gets a firm hold on it. I was nipped and scratched a number of times but never had a finger crushed. After lobstering for a few years, you became very adept at handling them quickly with your hands, fingers and anticipated their actions better.

After finishing a day of lobstering, any lobsters not eaten that night were stored in the keeper pot, from which they couldn't escape. A keeper pot was a normal lobster pot that was stripped of all the internal netting and the entrances and escape vents were covered with wire. There was no way they could get out. One of my buoys was fastened to it and after putting in the surplus lobsters, it was dropped in the ocean and stayed there until the next time we needed lobsters.

Before lobstering we needed bait for twenty pots. Ten were Dad's and ten were mine. During the Summer we caught enough flounder and cod for bait. In the Spring and Fall, to save time to work on the cottage, Dad would stop at a fish market in Worcester. There he bought cod heads and frames, which filled a five-gallon bucket.

As the price kept increasing, I arranged with the owner of a nearby fish market to pick up one five-gallon bucket a week at no charge. The owner of the market had to pay a trash removal company to dispose of the fish remains after he cleaned them. He arranged with a number of small time lobstermen to pick up a bucket or two of bait each week and thus reduce his trash removal costs. This arrangement lasted until the day I stopped lobstering. We both saved money.

Dad and I read every article and story we could find about lobstering, always looking for something that would help increase the catch or make it easier. We soaked the bait in various liquids and used canned cat foot put in white plastic containers with holes drilled in them. We bought large pots that had two separate parlors with separate bait overhanging the tapered nets on both sides. The large pots produced more lobsters, but they were much heavier and harder to pull, particularly during rough weather. Nothing worked better than freshly caught bait. Bluefish was the best and mackerel second.

We would start lobstering in mid May, East of The Gurnet. From there the lobsters would move into the big rocks near The Gurnet. The largest rocks would show up on low tides. The most dangerous were those just under the water surface. The closer you were to the shore, the better the lobstering. There was always a fear that if anything happened, both you and the boat could be thrown against the rocks. The boat and motor would be smashed and what would happen to you is unknown. The motor was left running in neutral when you were amongst the rocks, pulling your pots. You were always ready to make a quick getaway if needed.

In the middle of the Summer, the lobsters would migrate to the weed beds just off Saquish Beach where they would molt and stay for a couple of months. Sometimes they would molt inside your pot where, for a couple of days, the old shell was still hard and intact. The molted lobsters were much larger and softer than the old shell. It would take a couple of weeks for their shells to harden. Those that molted in the weed beds would then go on a feeding spree. In the late summer a few pots were placed on the sand bars in the deeper water beyond the weed beds. At night some razor clams would stick up out of the sand and the newly molted lobsters would feed on them and then hide in the sand until the following night.

During the peak of the Summer season some commercial lobstermen would place a number of their pot lines in the weed beds just off our beach. The pot lines consisted of ten pots connected one to another by a heavy rope. The last pot on each end of the line would have a smaller rope connected to a buoy. If one of the buoys were cut by a motorboat, the 10 pots could be retrieved by using the other buoy.

A pulley was used to retrieve their pots. Each was opened, lobsters and by product catch removed, then re-baited and stacked in order in the back of the boat. After the last one in the line was stacked, the boat would then move in a line that was parallel to the shore and the first pot was pushed over the side. Each of the nine remaining pots were automatically pulled in by the preceding pot and rope. Every now and then a commercial line crossed one of our lines between our buoy and our pot. The water was shallow, yet it was still an effort to pull the pot up and untangle the lines.

A commercial lobsterman had between two and six hundred pots on lines in deep water beyond The Gurnet. He would pull one half of the pots every other day. Fresh bait and two nights in the water made for an optimum catch. During a warm calm day, they worked in ideal conditions. During a cold, rainy day or before and after a major storm, it was just the opposite. These lobstermen would head out early in the morning when the weather was calm and return by mid to late afternoon. They lobstered ten months of the year, April through January. The remaining two months were spent repairing their equipment and getting ready for the next season.

When a major storm or hurricane was imminent, they brought their pots out further into deeper water where the turbulence was not as bad and the pots might remain on the ocean bottom with less disturbance. If time permitted, they were brought to shore and stored were they would be safe from the anticipated storm. If the pots were left in shallower water, once the turbulence started the pot lines moving, they would tangle with one another. The pots would then be crushed by rolling on the ocean floor. In a major storm, a lobsterman could lose most or all of his pots, worth many thousands of dollars. This coupled with the fact that he would not be catching any lobsters for a decent amount of time, doubled the financial disaster.

The storms also had an impact on the recreational lobstermen at Saquish. Some pots washed onto the beach and were easy to retrieve. Others tangled with the commercial lines and were crushed. Still others were carried to Western Point and thrashed against the rocks, or were carried into Duxbury Bay. Some just disappeared forever, never to be found. Besides the storms, a couple of lines between the buoys and pots were cut by motorboats every year. Lobstering was not an inexpensive activity, but for those of us that did it, lobstering was challenging, exciting and enjoyable.

When we started lobstering, Ann and the girls would draw a matrix showing each pot number (the buoys were numbered 0-9) and the date we pulled them. The number of lobsters caught in each pot was then recorded for that date. This proved very informative in determining how many lobsters were caught in each pot for the year. Some pots were very good, some were average and some were bad. Before the next season you would try to enhance the bad producing pots by tightening the nets and making other adjustments. In general very good pots stayed good, average pots stayed average and bad pots stayed bad. After a couple of years, the bad pots were replaced with new ones. Every now and then a bad pot would return to average. In retrospect the time spent in trying to improve bad pots was not worth the effort.

After catching a lobster you measured it with a gauge, which was hooked to the back of the eye socket and if the hard shell extended beyond the length of the gauge, it was a keeper. If not you threw it back. Next you turned the keeper over to see if little black eggs were attached to its stomach. If there were, it was an egg bearing female and was thrown back into the ocean.

Over the years, the length of the gauge and escape vents were increased. It later was required to cut a V shaped notch in the tail of an egg bearing female. With the notch, it was illegal to have one in your possession, whether or not eggs were present. This was incorporated in the state statutes to help manage and increase the lobster population.

After a few years we were catching all the lobsters we wanted, and asked the Fish and Game Department of Massachusetts, if both Dad and I could use the same ten pots.

Our colors were the same and both I.D. numbers would be burnt into the buoys and pots.

They checked and told us there was nothing in the state statutes that prohibited this. It would also result in fewer caught lobsters so they said it was O.K. It also resulted in our time, effort and expense being cut in half. Of course we only caught half as many lobsters, but that was all we needed.

Game wardens were a rarity in the lobstering grounds. I was checked by a warden three times. Once was when I was putting lobsters into the keeper pot which had more than twenty lobsters already in it. He checked every one for size and eggs. None had shrunk in size, so they all passed.

One of the articles I read gave instructions on how to hypnotize lobsters. You turned them over and laid them on their backs while pinning their claws to the ground. Then you would rub their belly for a minute, turn them over, tuck their tail underneath them and stand them on their tail.

They would then stand there as if completely hypnotized. I practiced doing this for a number of times and found out that each time it was done the lobster would stay in the trance for roughly the same amount of time. Then it would just collapse and fall on its stomach.

Shortly after reading the article, the Halls and Gallos with their children came to visit us for a weekend. After bringing in a catch of lobsters, I told all the kids about my magic hypnotic powers. How I would turn the lobsters on their backs, rub their bellies while saying some magic words (that I made up) and stand them on their tails. Then whenever I wanted to take them out of the spell I would clap my hands and within a few seconds the lobster would collapse. I had it down to a science. It worked like a charm and they were all excited, amazed and impressed. Maureen Hall still remembers that as the very top of her Saquish memories. I never tried to hypnotize anything else, lobster were enough.

During my lobstering career I had a host of pleasant, enjoyable memories. The most dominant memory however was a life-threatening situation. In the Summer of 1983 Ann, Lorri and I were at Saquish for a vacation. Kathi was in high school and had a summer job so she stayed in Westboro. Ann's mother, Anna had ovarian cancer and her health was deteriorating. Ann gave her mother's neighbor, the Coast Guard telephone number at Saquish. In an emergency the Coast Guard would deliver a message to us.

The Coast Guard had a barracks near The Gurnet Lighthouse and was still patrolling the entrance to Plymouth Harbor and Cape Cod Bay. One morning a Coast Guard vehicle stopped in front of the cottage and two Coast Guard men came to the door. Ann's mother had been rushed to the hospital. Ann immediately left for Connecticut leaving Lorri and me at Saquish. After she saw her mother she would let us know how her mother was doing.

It was a warm sunny morning, a perfect day to be out in my boat. I decided to pull my lobster pots which were just off The Gurnet. Six lobsters were caught that morning and coming back across the bay I had the throttle wide open. The ocean was as calm as a mirror. The boat was going about 25 MPH. I was in somewhat of a daze and all of a sudden my lobster gauge fell off the seat in front of me. Subconsciously I lunged to grab it, taking my hand off the motor steering handle. The motor immediately turned 90 degrees and so did the boat.

I continued to go straight ahead and into the water. It took place so fast that I found myself under the water, not immediately realizing what had happened. I knew however there was a boat and motor with a sharp revolving propeller somewhere above me. I held my breath as long as possible, could just hear a muffled sound but nothing else, ran out of breath and had to surface.

After surfacing, I saw the boat going in a circle but heading right at me. My first instinct was to grab the side of the boat and try to swing up over the side. If this was not successful, falling back over the side might have resulted in my legs being ripped up by the propeller. In a split second I made a decision to paddle backwards still facing the boat and thrust my legs away from the propeller as my shoulders and head leaned toward the boat. The propeller missed my legs by inches.

Before the next pass I was able to paddle backwards, a couple of feet away from the circling boat. My boots were filled with water and it felt like weights were tied around my ankles trying to pull me down. Then I submerged, reached down, took off one boot and let it sink to the ocean bottom. I surfaced again and on its next pass the boat was now a few feet away from me. I then submerged again and took off the second boot. Upon surfacing I felt somewhat safe, as the circling boat was further away. I turned around in the water and started to swim toward shore, constantly looking back over my shoulder to continuously check on the boat's location.

The swim to shore was less than a mile, but before going very far two men that were fishing for flounder saw what happened. They started their boat, pulled up their anchor, came to my rescue and helped me climb into their boat. The question was how to stop my boat that was still going around in circles. We decided to make our way close to the boat and the fisherman sitting in front would grab on to the boat and slow it down long enough for me to swing over the side and into the boat. When he grabbed the boat, however, the motor immediately stopped. After slipping over the side into the boat and reaching into my lobster container, they received the six lobsters as a thank you. I then went back to the cottage, took a warm shower, went outside to sit in the sun on the porch and then started to shiver. I don't know how many flounder they caught, but I'm sure their spouses enjoyed the lobsters more than the flounder. They must have had an interesting story to tell. Good spouses would never accuse you of stopping at a fish market to buy lobsters and creating a made up story, unless you hadn't caught any flounder!

I didn't mention any thing about this event to Ann until the time was right to sit down and tell her the whole story. She had just lost her mother and the thought of almost losing her best friend and lover at the same time would have been overwhelming. She still shivered and cried each time she read and reread about it while we were working on the writing of this story.

On the other hand, one of my fondest memories relates to my first grandson Cory. He loved to go lobstering whenever he visited Saquish. He would go with me along with Ann or his mother.

When he was four years old, I made him a small lobster buoy with my colors on it and attached it to a 12' piece of rope. I bought him a pair of small lobster gloves and a pail. We put some pegs and a lobster gauge inside the pail. This was his very own lobstering gear and he took it with him each time we went lobstering.

When I seized a lobster buoy and started to pull in a pot, he would throw his lobster buoy overboard and then pull it back with the rope. He never caught any lobsters, but sure had many fun filled days. With this initial experience Cory is now a great helper for his dad Brian with their recreational lobstering efforts on Nantucket Island.

One day he was with me when a 28" striped bass was in the pot. The only one ever caught that way. It must have chased a sand crab and it was the first legal size striper that Cory caught.

In the first decade of the twenty-first century major storms covered the weed beds that were in front of the cottage with sand. With no place to molt, the lobsters were no longer coming to the Front Bay. As the weed beds have started to return, the lobstering is improving.

During the thirty-five years of lobstering, I caught over seven thousand keeper lobsters. Many more than that were shorts and were thrown back. Large numbers of short lobsters were always a good sign for the next few years.

Every time a pot was opened you had no idea what if anything was inside. Along with lobsters, there were a number of quaint surprises. Spider crabs, moon shells and flounder were quite frequent. Every now and then cod, sea robins, scalpin, skate, fluke and tautog were there. We caught many more sand crabs than lobsters. The surprise of a large lobster was, more often than not, offset by the discovery it was an egg bearing female.

One time when approaching a buoy, the buoy was moving around in the water. A bluefish with a large plug hooked in its mouth had broken a fishing line. One of the treble hooks that were attached to the plug then became entangled in my lobster buoy line. That was the only bluefish I caught with my lobster gear, however it was not trapped in my pot.

The most lobsters kept in one pull was eighteen. The biggest one we could keep was three and one half pounds. The total shell was displayed by hanging it on our fish net in the den. The biggest lobster ever caught was an egg-bearing female in the very last pot pulled at the end of my lobstering career. Since it was an egg bearing female it was released. Unfortunately we didn't have a camera with us to take a picture nor did we have a scale to weigh it.

All the company that visited us at Saquish had never experienced lobstering. They would quickly learn how to haul the pots up and experience the thrill of catching one or more lobsters. The last pot that they pulled was the keeper pot.

They had no idea that this was any different from any other pot. I assured them that this pot would catch more lobsters than any other one had. It was amazing to see the excited shock and pleasant surprise when they hauled the pot into the boat. The next question I asked was, "How many lobsters would you like for dinner this evening?"

Many of our visiting friends recall lobstering as the most memorable event of their Saquish experience.

LOBSTERING

CHAPTER 12

STRIPED BASS AND BLUEFISH

During the early seventies, fishing in Duxbury, Plymouth, Kingston and Cape Cod Bay for stripers was excellent. In the mid-seventies bluefish started to show up in large numbers and stripers started to decline. An old time fisherman once told me that when the eel grass disappeared from the bays the stripers also would. Coincidently or not that's what happened.

The size restriction on stripers was in the teens and there was no limit on how many you could keep. In the late seventies or early eighties, a restriction was placed on stripers. You could keep only one fish that was 36" or longer. Any fish that was shorter than that had to be released. Fish over that size were breeding females, so to the lay person this did not make sense. Over the next number of years, the size was decreased to 32" then to 30" and finally 28". The number you could keep was increased to two per day, and the number of stripers did keep increasing.

Stripers would migrate from the Chesapeake Bay all the way to Maine. Each state had its own statutes regarding how many you could keep and of what length. This applied to both commercial and recreational fishing. Even though the numbers of stripers have increased, they are nowhere near the numbers of the early seventies.

Bluefish, which were not seen in the local waters, and menhaden both arrived in large numbers at about the same time. Menhaden are bait fish that grow to a foot long. Both stripers and blues devour them. Stripers only use them for food, but blues will go on a killing spree and with their razor sharp teeth will take a bite out of one and then continue on to chomp on many more.

One Summer when the menhaden schools were at their peak, the blues arrived in large numbers. A killing spree lasted for a couple of days. For the next few days, tens if not hundreds of thousands of dead menhaden washed up onto Saquish and the surrounding beaches and shoreline.

At the high tide level, the continuous pile of dead menhaden was two to three feet tall. Paths were shoveled so that vehicles could cross from the beach to the sand above the high tide level. The intense aroma of decaying menhaden lasted for two weeks.

The commercial fishing industry found a new source of revenue using menhaden for cat food. As a result, the number of menhaden rapidly decreased. So did the blues, although there are still decent amounts of them in the bay. It just takes a lot more effort to catch them.

We fished mostly with surface plugs and swimmers. Menhaden, cut mackerel, large sea clams and sea worms were seldom used. Even though live or cut bait was very effective for large bass, sitting and waiting was boring for us. It must have been our dedication to fly casting for trout that prompted us to use spinning rods for stripers. Fly casting for salt water fish was not popular in the early seventies. For some reason trolling never interested either Dad or me.

Casting and slowly retrieving live eels was effective for medium size bass in the ten to twenty-pound range and every now and then we would use live eels for bait. But to see and feel a bass or blue smash a surface plug was the most exciting of all.

The Striper Swiper and Rebel Swimmer caught the most bass. Of course we fished them the most. The Reverse Atom, a large surface plug with three treble hooks caught the most large (over twenty pounds) bass. It was a squid imitation and resembled a brown beer bottle pulled forward.

A large bass would roll right alongside of the plug and smash it with its tail, sending up a spray of water. It would then turn around and in a couple of seconds engulf the plug. Once you learned what was happening and adjusted, you hooked close to 100% of the hits.

After seeing the large splash, you had to wait until the line started to leave the reel. Only then would you set the hook. This knowledge was acquired once a large striper doubled back and chased the plug. The patience to wait the few short seconds, which seemed like an eternity, was a different matter.

One fall weekend during the bass migration, Gene Wojnar, his son Mark and I fished for two days in the Back Bay. On both Saturday and Sunday we caught over seventy school size bass each day. These were bass that were big enough to keep, but weighed less than a couple of pounds. It took as much time to clean them as it took to catch them. However, we had enough fish for every Friday evening until the following Spring.

When we arrived one Friday, we heard reports that stripers had congregated in the ocean side of High Pines. Early Saturday, Gene and Dad joined me in my twelve-foot boat and we went around The Gurnet toward High Pines.

With three men in the boat and only a twelve horsepower motor, the going was very slow. We didn't see a sign of any seagulls diving or fish breaking the water. After passing High Pines we saw a large flock of seagulls on the Duxbury Bay side of the beach. A large school of stripers were chasing bait fish to the surface and the sea gulls were splashing into the water all over the place. They were having a feast on the wounded and crippled bait fish, and we were on the wrong side of the peninsula over ten miles away from them by sea.

It would take considerable time to circle around The Gurnet, Western Point, Clark's Island and into Duxbury Bay, to cover the ten mile distance to reach them. It was near high tide and the distance across Duxbury Beach from the ocean side to the bay was about 150 yards. We decided it was quicker to take the motor off the boat, have one of us carry it while the other two carried the boat and fishing equipment. It only took fifteen minutes to make the portage over the beach and into Duxbury Bay, but it was an exhausting trip with numerous stops to rest and recuperate. The stripers and seagulls continued their activity, resulting in a successful but tired morning.

In the Fall, a couple of years later, a number of us were drifting in Duxbury Bay in Goose's boat on a warm, sunny afternoon. The women were sunbathing and the men were casting into a school of migrating stripers. I hooked an undersized striper and had it halfway to the boat. All of a sudden the line went slack. When the line was retrieved, on the plug was one half of a small striped bass. We could only figure that there was a decent size shark in the bay that had bitten the striper in half and we had never seen anything like it before.

Early one morning the following Summer, Dad and I headed for Western Point to fish for stripers. When we arrived, the rip was boiling with decent sized fish smashing the surface. As we circled around and drifted back through them, we both hooked fish. Before we could land them we saw many more swimming right around the boat. They were much bigger than the average striped bass, and were a fish we had never seen before. We landed ten large bluefish each close to twelve pounds. As best we could determine, these were the first bluefish caught in the Saquish Beach area. Evidently the fish that decapitated my small striper the previous Fall was likely a forerunner of the bluefish species.

We started using eight-pound test line. Large bass broke it three times. It wasn't like freshwater fishing. Two of them circled and doubled back under the boat. The other rolled over and cut the line with its scales. One of them was very big. Not only did you lose a large fish, but you lost a plug that cost quite a few bucks. From there the line was changed to twelve and finally fifteen-pound test. No more big fish were lost on broken lines.

The best bass fishing was at Western Point about one to two hours after the high tide. It was excellent when the seagulls were there diving for the wounded bait fish. The second best was chasing diving seagulls wherever they were. Terns would frequently circle and dive into the water. Often, however, they were just chasing bait fish. That's why they acquired the nickname "Liar Terns." If no seagulls were diving, Duxbury Bay was the best for blind casting. For some reason we never spent much time fishing in Kingston or Plymouth Bays, although I'm sure the fishing was just as good. However, if we saw sea gulls diving in the bays we would chase after them and often were successful.

In early June, large bass would follow the mackerel as they migrated into Cape Cod Bay. At this time, the rip at Western Point would provide some very large bass. During the Summers, blues would often chase the bait fish right up onto Saquish as the migrating schoolies would do in the fall. When this happened you could do very well fishing right off the beach, often directly in front of the cottage.

When the blues were feeding, they would strike anything, and you caught them in large numbers. Bass were caught in much smaller numbers. Even when they were in schools, an approaching motorboat would scare the bass. The school would dive down, disappear and then they would reappear in a different location. Sometimes you could chase the schools for long periods of time, but they were so jittery they would continually dive and disappear just before you reached them. If you were the only boat, you could sneak up on them at a slow speed with little noise. Once there were a number of boats, it was a race to see who could get there first, and the first boat might hook a fish before they dove and disappeared.

One year, the day before the 4th of July, people coming to Saquish told us a large school of bluefish were chasing mackerel up onto Duxbury Beach. This was right in front of High Pines. A number of us jumped into our vehicles and drove onto the beach at High Pines. The blues were breaking on top of the water and when a wave broke a number of mackerel would come up onto the beach. People were running around picking them up and putting them in plastic bags. The mackerel that had washed up on the previous wave would swim back out on the next wave and new mackerel would wash onto the beach. Those that were bitten by the blues would wash in and stay on the beach. They were pushed further up onto the beach with each additional breaking wave.

We started to cast and on every cast you hooked a bluefish averaging about eight pounds. After catching four bluefish I hooked a much heavier and stronger fish than what we were catching. It would come in, about two breakers from the beach, then turned around and took line off my reel.

This happened a number of times until it finally made the first breaker and was guided up onto the shore. It turned out to be a thirty-three pound striped bass. When I cleaned it, there were three full size mackerel in its stomach. It was having a feast on mackerel that the blues had already wounded or killed.

During the better fishing time for blues, I was working professionally for Brendon Healey. We frequently talked about bluefish. I had caught quite a number and he had never caught one, even though he owned a large boat and had done a fair amount of fishing in the Quincy Bay area, which was near Boston Harbor. On a summer day I had scheduled a managers meeting at my Saquish cottage and invited Brendon to join us.

It was a beautiful calm day and while driving out over Duxbury Beach to meet them, I stopped, rolled down the window and had a feeling that this was a day for bluefish. Whether it was the different smell in the air or just intuition and experience, who knows. I always carried a collapsible spinning rod in the SUV. My managers had two four wheel drives and after meeting everyone we started back down the beach. When we arrived in front of High Pines I noticed two dead menhaden on the beach. We stopped the vehicles and everyone stepped out. The managers were standing around talking up a storm and just enjoying the pleasant morning on a remote, barren beach. I picked up a dead menhaden and threw it under hand, as far as I could, into the open ocean. It no sooner hit the water and started to sink when there was a big swirl in the water. For some reason no one else noticed it.

After retrieving the spinning rod from the SUV, putting a plug on the line and heaving it as far out as possible, I handed the rod to Brendon and told him to start reeling as fast as he could. No sooner had he taken three or four turns of the reel, when the water exploded. His first bluefish and over twelve pounds. The managers then took turns casting and catching blues.

I drove back to the cottage and retrieved two more spinning rods. Everyone caught as many blues as they wanted. The water would continuously boil up with breaking fish and then quiet down. This lasted well into the afternoon. A number of people from Duxbury, including a reporter, showed up and there was an article that appeared in the next week's local paper. The highlight of the day was that one of the managers caught an eighteen-pound bluefish, the biggest one I have ever seen. Not much work was accomplished at the meeting that day.

Early on a fall morning, Mark Wojnar woke me and said the blues were crashing the beach right in front of the cottage. I jumped out of bed, grabbed my spinning rod and ran down to the beach without putting on any boots. An hour later, after catching a number of blues, my feet were frozen from standing in the cold water. After going back to the cottage and soaking them in hot water, I went back to bed and slept for a couple of hours. Then I woke, had breakfast and went back to catch more blues. This time I wore boots and the blues stayed close to shore for half the day.

Another time Mark and a friend of his caught a very large number of blues just off the beach. They took them to Plymouth and sold them to a restaurant for ten cents a pound. Doesn't sound like much, but more than twenty-five years ago, for two young boys with a boat full of blues, it was a fair amount of money. Gas for the motor boat was relatively cheap then, just like the price of bluefish.

During the peak time of striper fishing, if we caught a number of medium to good size fish, Gene and I would go to Plymouth and sell them to a fish wholesaler who had a refrigerator truck right on the pier. He paid between fifty cents to a dollar per pound on the hoof. There was one time when he paid a maximum of two dollars per pound. Not a way to make a living, but for two young guys on vacation it provided some decent spending money.

For a few years of our striper fishing endeavors, Danny Keegan and I joined the American Littoral Society headquartered in Sandy Hook, New Jersey. They provided tags and post cards to record striped bass information. Each time you caught a striper and before it was released, you inserted a numbered and addressed tag under the fish's back fin. A post card had the tag number printed on it. You filled in the date caught, location released, approximate weight and length. You then signed the tag and sent it to New Jersey.

When someone caught a tagged fish, they would remove the tag and send it to the same address with the same type of information you had initially provided. This helped with managing the species by providing migration patterns and changes in weight and length.

Each time one of your tagged fish was caught, you were informed where and when it was caught including changes in weight and length. Of all the fish Danny and I tagged, we received three notifications of second catches, all were more than a year later. One was in Kingston Bay, near where it was initially caught. The other two were caught in the Chesapeake Bay, a major breeding area for stripers. Naturally, they had all increased in length and weight.

My Uncle Steve was quite a fisherman. While visiting us, one day he went fishing with Gene and they chased a large school of blues into Kingston Bay. Steve had the very unique experience of catching two blues on one plug at the same time. Evidently they were either vicious or hungry that day. It had nothing to do with Steve's fishing ability or Gene's experience as a fishing guide.

That Summer we heard that the blues were heavily concentrated about five miles across the bay right in front of the nuclear power plant. Water was drawn from the ocean and pumped into the power plant to cool the nuclear reactors.

It then was pumped back into the bay. The returning water was much warmer than when it was extracted from the bay. At times it flowed back into the bay with the volume of a river.

When the electric company was applying for construction permits to build the plant, environmentalists were saying that the discharge would pollute the bay and kill all the fish and lobsters. Just the opposite happened. The discharged warm water created a temperature gradient. Large numbers of baitfish would accumulate in front of the power plant and attract blues, stripers and lobsters.

On a calm Saturday Richard Balakier, Dad and I took our fourteen-foot aluminum boat, made the five-mile trip into Plymouth Harbor, snagged a number of menhaden then made the five-mile jaunt from Plymouth Harbor to the power plant.

We caught many blues, but with three men in a fourteen-foot boat and a twenty-five horsepower engine, the trip took a fair amount of time. Before we went back the next day, Richard had a great idea. We took his twenty-five horsepower motor and placed it on the boat right next to our motor. Then it was locked in place so it could not be moved from side to side and therefore it was only used for straight ahead power. Our motor was used for steering control and straight ahead power. On a calm ocean it worked very well and substantially increased our speed. We used this idea of twin-engines a number of times that Summer. This was the first time we heard or knew of the twin-engine idea. It was solely Richard's idea but he never did anything with it. Might have missed out on making a bundle of money, or it might have been a wild-goose chase that cost him a bundle. You never know!

One morning when I was fishing alone in Duxbury Bay, a large thick fog bank accumulated in front of Saquish Beach. Duxbury Bay remained as clear as could be. Normally I would return between seven and eight o'clock. This day the fog was so thick that I decided to wait it out. Around ten o'clock Ann and Richard came looking for me and all of a sudden their boat broke out of the fog into the clear Duxbury Bay. They were very concerned that I was lost in the fog. I appreciated that they were concerned about me. However, if Duxbury Bay was as fogged in as Saquish, we all would have been lost in the fog. "Where in the fog are we."

While on vacation, I would quite often take a spin in the boat looking for stripers. One day when I was out behind Clark's Island, a strong, fast wind suddenly blew in from the Southwest. It was an incoming tide and before I reached the channel between Western Point and Clark's Island the breakers were three to four feet high, with very little room between them.

I initially started to make a run close to Western Point, then decided the boat would not get through and it might get tipped over. A quick 90 degree turn, between the breakers, put the boat onto the sandy beach inside of Western Point. The anchor was placed high up on the sand and I walked back to the cottage. After the tide receded, I used the truck and boat trailer to retrieve the boat.

Another time there was a considerable wind blowing from the North. With Saquish Beach facing due South, very little surf was in front of the cottage. I decided to go around The Gurnet to Duxbury Beach and do some striper fishing. It was an incoming tide and as I rounded The Gurnet, there were waves four feet high and the boat was quickly caught between them. One large wave hit the front of the boat and lifted it into the air. As soon as it came down, I instinctively made a quick three hundred and sixty degree turn and somehow stayed safely between two waves for the short distance back around The Gurnet. There the wind which was blocked by The Gurnet was much less intense in both height and severity. I easily made it back to the cottage and didn't start to shiver until standing on the porch and thinking about what might have happened. I'm not sure how these maneuvers were possible without having help from above.

If the waves had capsized the boat, I might well have been thrown up against the sharp rocks and large boulders that were in front of The Gurnet. This time and the time I flipped out of the boat while lobstering were the two most frightening and life-threatening experiences I had in the forty years. During these times I never wore a life preserver vest when fishing or lobstering in the inshore waters. Nobody else did. When we went out cod fishing in the deeper waters, it was the only time we wore them. As time passed and we grew older and smarter, life preserver vests were worn much more frequently.

On a Sunday afternoon, Dad and I were striper fishing off Western Point. It was quite late in the afternoon and we were just drifting. All of a sudden, a good sized boat came around Western Point and was heading right at us. The driver was headed into the setting sun and was blinded by it. Dad stood up, yelled and waved his hands. The driver saw him just in time to turn and sideswiped our boat. Thankfully he did not hit us head on, which would have created a disaster. Dad used some of the strongest language I have ever heard him use, but the boat keep going and nobody else but I could hear him.

Sandy Wojnar's father had done a fair amount of striper fishing off the beaches of Cape Cod. We were fishing in Duxbury Bay one morning and caught a number of schoolies. While unhooking one of them, the fish slipped out of my hands and one of the treble hooks penetrated my finger beyond the barb. The two of us stabilized the fish on the bottom of the boat and unhooked it.

Next we used a sharp jackknife to cut a slice in my finger right next to the hook.

It was deep enough to lift out the barb. This saved us a trip to the Emergency Room at the Jordan Hospital in Plymouth that would have taken a much longer time, but might have been less painful.

On the way in, her father commented on the number of fish that we caught, and talked about the larger fish he had caught off the Cape Cod beaches. He mentioned about never seeing a large striper taken out of the Plymouth area. When we arrived back at Saquish, Phil Rawinski had just returned from fishing the Plymouth Harbor channel with live menhaden. He had two stripers that weighed well over forty pounds. Enough said about the location of large stripers.

The first weekend that the Halls and Gallos visited us, Dave, Frank and I went striper fishing before daybreak on Saturday morning. The conditions were right to fish the rip at Western Point. On one of the first drifts, I caught a bass that weighed twenty pounds. A few drifts later Dave Hall hooked another bass. The boat was drifting with the tide and Dave's fish was running against it. Dave yelled that the line was quickly leaving his reel. I had adjusted the drags the night before so everything should have been all right. We were using fifteen pound test line. Twice I reached down and tightened the drag a little. The rod bent over a little more each time but the receding line did not slow down.

I started the engine, turned the boat around and continued fast enough to keep pressure on the fish and let Dave put line back on the reel. We chased the fish one more time. Then Dave was able to gain more line than the fish was able to take off the real in each additional run that the fish made. Many people that have fished for stripers have never caught one. On Dave's first attempt at striper fishing the fish that he landed weighed thirty-four pounds. Some people are lucky, others are not!

Once while fishing at the bass hole in front of The Gurnet, Gene and I heard a loud splash in back of the boat. A large bass had broken water. In the next minute it rolled over two more times as we watched. It was the largest bass we had ever seen and estimated it was well over fifty pounds. It was chasing live bait and would not hit any of the plugs that we tried.

During an early August morning in 1985, Gene and I were fishing an outgoing tide at the Western Point rip. On the third drift Gene saw a large bass chase his Rebel Swimmer right up to the boat. On the next drift we both hooked onto large fish. We had to keep the lines from tangling together or wrapping around the propeller as both large bass ran from side to side. Next we had to avoid the lobster buoys as the boat drifted beyond the rip.

Since we both had fish hooked, neither one of us could start the engine and maneuver the boat to clear the buoys. Luckily by the time we reached them, both fish had sounded and we kept them close to the boat until we passed through the buoys. With fifteen pound test line you were very cautious to keep it from breaking and years of experience proved helpful. We landed both fish and even though we knew that a school of large bass had just arrived at the rip, our fishing was done for the day, since the regulations then allowed for one bass over 36" per person, per day. These were the biggest stripers we had ever caught. We then went back to Saquish, put the bass in the SUV and drove to Plymouth to have them weighed. My bass weighed forty-four pounds, Gene's forty-seven, and his was entered into the contest for the largest striped bass caught in Massachusetts waters for the year 1985. It didn't win a prize, but it was the most exciting day of fishing we ever had.

It's not catching bass that I remember the most. It was leaving the cottage before sunrise during calm mornings, then drifting with the outgoing tide and watching the sun rise up out of the ocean. It always was a pleasant, peaceful and rewarding experience, a chance to be in touch with your Creator. If a bass or two were caught, that just made it a more pleasant morning.

MEDIUM SIZE STRIPED BASS

CHAPTER 13

THE PRIESTS FROM MIRAMAR

During our first weekend at Saquish, while visiting the Wojnar's, we went to a Mass presided over by Father Reed, a priest from the Divine Word Missionaries. The Divine Word has a seminary in Duxbury named Miramar and it overlooks Kingston Bay. There they trained missionaries that preached in many remote places in the world.

In 1962 Jack Ruprecht, a major landowner on the beach, received permission from the Bishop to have priests from the Divine Word Order say Mass at Saquish. Permission was granted based on the remoteness of the Saquish location. For the priests, it was a very short distance to travel compared with many of the remote places they served. Saying Mass at Saquish didn't even require them to stay overnight, as much of their missionary work required. Usually it wasn't just over night, but it extended for a year or more.

That Saturday afternoon, Father Reed came in a four wheel drive pick up truck, the cargo area of which was filled with young adults. Some of them even had guitars. It was the first Folk Mass we attended.

Initially the Mass was said on the back road behind the Devir's cottage. Due to the Blizzard of '78, the location was damaged and the Mass location was moved to the beach in front of the Bien's cottage. Later it was relocated to the top of the sand dune in front of the Balakier's cottage. When it rained, which was seldom, it was held underneath the Bien's cottage or under Balakier's back porch, both of which were protected from the rain. During a couple of rainy days, it was even held in our cottage, once downstairs and once in the observation room.

A church committee controlled the disbursement of church funds which were collected at Mass. Fifty dollars was given to the priest that said Mass and anything over that was put into an account to build a church. Jack Ruprecht was responsible for handling the Mass kit, which was a suitcase that contained an altar stone, chalice, cruets, Bible, hosts and vestments the priest wore when saying Mass.

He also arranged for the parishioners to provide the priests with transportation to and from Duxbury, and to host them for dinner. Every now and then he would drive up to our front steps and come in to see us. He left his wife and dog siting in the SUV waiting for him. Ann would always ask Jack to bring his wife into the cottage, but his reply was that he was not staying very long, which usually turned out to be misleading.

His stops always entailed discussions with Ann about some aspect of Mass coordination. She always told him what she thought, even though it was not what he always wanted to hear. Ann had gained his respect. One day he stopped and told her he was no longer able to take care of the transportation for the priests or the handling of the Mass kit, and wanted Ann to take care of them. Ann accepted responsibility for the Mass kit and Sandy Wojnar took the responsibility for recruiting people to transport the priests and host them for dinner. Plymouth already had decided to stop issuing new building permits at Saquish so the balance in the church fund and the total collection from Mass was turned over to Miramar and the church committee was abolished.

The Divine Word Missionaries had a unique way of saying Mass. It was compact and the homilies were said in short simplistic terms, but would deliver a clear significant message to which everyone could relate. The young children, especially our Lorri, would sit there and often play in the sand but when the homily started they would snap to attention. After Mass it was very enjoyable to host the priests for dinner. Father Wong was the first priest we knew very well. Every now and then he would stop at our home in Westboro to visit us, often spending a couple of hours and staying for dinner.

As the number of priests entering the seminary was declining, Father Paul Connors was placed in control of Miramar, with the objective of stabilizing it financially. He closed the Seminary, sold off a part of the properties that became condominiums, and converted the operation into a retreat facility for both religious and lay people. We became very close to Father Connors and besides the long intensive discussions at dinner after Mass, he would come to visit us at other times, often bringing some of his religious friends who were making retreats at Miramar.

When the Coast Guard was closing down operation of the lighthouse, Father Connors tried to buy Gurnet Light as a supplemental retreat location, but was not successful. He was able however, to arrange for Miramar to acquire a four-wheel drive truck. Its main purpose was for snow plowing at the Miramar facility, but secondarily it provided the priests with their own transportation to and from Saquish for the Saturday Mass. This meant parishioners only had to host the priest for dinner on Saturday evening, and no longer had to provide the two round trips to Duxbury Beach,

Four years after my Mother passed away, Dad met Alice and they decided to marry. Dad and the pastor of his church had different understandings pertaining to a new church regulation regarding lessons before marriage. We talked with Father Connors and he offered to check with the Bishop's Office in Boston. Within one week the situation was resolved in Dad's favor.

Father Connors was later followed by Father Bob Jones. He participated as actively in Saquish and its activities as Father Connors had. For a number of years, Father Bob joined us for dinner a number of times each year. After dinner we and some of our friends would sit around the table with him and discuss the issues of the time. Many of these were serious issues and we had some in depth discussions that were enlightening.

When Lorri had her first child, she asked Kathi to be Cory's Godmother. Kathi had moved to San Francisco and was unable to make the trip to Nantucket for the date of the baptism. Kathi asked Ann to substitute for her. There was some confusion regarding the paperwork the church required to accomplish this. We talked to Father Bob and he offered to take care of it since he knew the Nantucket Pastor.

After the baptism Lorri and Brian had a cookout in their backyard. The Pastor, who attended the cook out, asked Ann how she knew Father Bob Jones. She told him about the relationship between Miramar and Saquish. The Pastor told us he had attended retreats at Miramar, knew Father Bob very well and thought highly of him.

After I retired, Father Bob found out that my pickup truck was left in back of the cottage when we went to Florida for the Winter. He suggested that I leave it at Miramar where there was less salty weather and there the truck would generate less rust. Staying there for the Winters, extended the life of the vehicle for a couple of years. It was a sad day when the truck finally rusted out and all the brake lines no longer functioned. It was then towed away and given to charity.

Kathi and Franz were married in San Francisco. Due to logistics, they were unable to have the ceremony conducted in their church. While they were vacationing at Saquish the following Summer, after a Saturday afternoon Mass, Father Bob held a private ceremony in front of our cottage. He blessed their marriage and made it official in the church by signing the appropriate documents. Susan Wojnar was the key witness.

I have related a number of personal experiences where Father Bob went out of his way to help us out. Many Saquish people could reiterate their personal experiences with him or other Miramar priests. They all are caring, giving priests consistent with their missionary background.

Over time the requirements for a Mass kit diminished. The altar stone was no longer required. The priests provided their own Mass items and vestments. All Saquish had to provide was the altar cloth, candles, candleholders and a collapsible altar. Initially Richard and Linda Balakier and then Sandy and Gene Wojnar took care of these items.

Most of the Masses are now said by three priests living at Miramar. They are Father Tom Griffith, Father Joe Connolly and Father Farley. In 2010 Father Connolly and Father Farley celebrated their 50th Year Anniversary as priests. In August 2012 Father Farley celebrated the 50th Year Anniversary Mass at Saquish, which from the start were consistently said on Saturday afternoons, a 50 year tradition.

It is hoped that the Divine Word Missionary priests from Miramar will continue to say the Saturday Mass at Saquish well into the future. Every friend of ours that attended one of the Masses, while visiting us, enjoyed the service and the short sermon that always made a point.

My heart felt thank you to all the Miramar priests that have ever said one or more Masses at Saquish. May God bless all of you.

CHAPTER 14

OUR PETS, JAKE, SPORT, SOX AND CASEY

When we bought the land at Saquish, Jake our short haired English Pointer was part of our family. Many of his adventures are found in Chapters 3 and 5 during the time we were building the cottage. He always enjoyed running up and down Saquish Beach, usually chasing sea gulls.

Jake's story however started a few years before. During our early hunting days Dad had a beagle that was an excellent hunting dog both for rabbits and pheasants. After the beagle passed away, Dad always wanted another hunting dog, but where they lived dogs were no longer allowed.

They moved to a new location where Dad and Mom were able to have a dog. Dad built a dog house and fenced in an area where the dog could live. Dad then looked all over and finally bought a one- year-old short haired English Pointer that he named Jake. Jake had quite a pedigree. On one side there were field champions and show champions were on the other. With this background, Dad was happy with his choice.

The only problem was that Jake was high strung and loved to run. He should have been a greyhound. When you went hunting, as soon as you opened the car door Jake would take off. He would disappear for about 2 hours, running over the hills and down the valleys and then all of a sudden he would reappear. Dad took him to a professional trainer, and both he and Dad went through an extensive training course. It helped a little, but Jake still did not respond well to commands. He was however a good hunter and even with our early morning frustrations with his behavior, by the end of the day our hunting was usually a success

About the time Ann, I and our two young daughters had returned from New Jersey and built a home in Westboro, Dad could no longer keep a dog where he was living. Ann and I were not ready for a pet even though the young girls would have loved one.

Dad, I and Ann's father, Peter Ben, were all members of a sporting club named the Singletary Rod and Gun Club. Dad and the club made an arrangement to sell chances for $1 a piece and have a raffle at one of its monthly meetings. Dad and the club would split the profit from the drawing and Dad committed to sell at least 100 tickets. By the time the drawing was held there were over 500 tickets sold. The winner of the raffle would own Jake. With his pedigree that was quite a prize for anyone who enjoyed pheasant hunting.

Dad tried to persuade Ann's father to buy $5 worth of tickets. Peter, even thought he was unlucky and had never won anything in a raffle, was reluctant to buy chances because he was not a hunter and wanted nothing to do with potentially owning a dog. I convinced him that his possibility of winning was minimal and if by a slim chance he won, Ann, Kathi, Lorri and I would take Jake. Sometimes your luck changes! Peter bought five chances, won the raffle and that is how Jake became a member of our family.

Even though he was a hunting dog and you could fire a shotgun right over his head without him flinching, he was extremely frightened by fireworks and thunderstorms. We think, but are not sure, that he might have been close to a misguided exploding skyrocket during one of the 4th of July celebrations on the beach. During these celebrations and thunderstorms he would crawl up on the floor near your legs and at night lie right next to our bed. He needed lots of love and attention, which we all gave him. Living in our home and at Saquish he became much more relaxed than he was living in an enclosed outside area. The need to take long runs decreased and his behavior changed. Jake was the love of the girls' lives. Lorri was not a doll lover, but she would dress Jake in baby clothes, just like he was her doll.

When the girls were young, we always spent Easter at Saquish. One year my parents wanted to give the girls two white bunnies for Easter. Dad had arranged to pick them up on Friday afternoon and bring them to the beach.

The girls would get them as a surprise on Easter morning. The rabbit breeder had forgotten about Dad's request and by Friday afternoon of Easter weekend all he had left was a pair of New Zealand red bunnies. Huge, huge bunnies! They were brought to Saquish and surreptitiously placed in the attic.

After the girls went to bed, Ann came out of our bedroom and a liquid that was dripping from the ceiling hit her right in the head. She didn't know what was happening and wondered what was causing it. She was not pleased when she found out. When you have to go you have to go. The huge bunnies really went and urinated much more than expected. It had flowed over the containment area in the cage, through the boards in the attic floor, then through the Knotty Pine ceiling in the hall and right on to Ann's head as she walked by. The bunnies were then moved into my parents' room.

Early Easter morning, the girls came out of their bedroom to look for their Easter baskets. My parents opened their door and released the bunnies. When the girls saw them they yelled. "The Easter Bunny left us bunnies!" To see the happiness on the girls' faces was a thrill for my parents.

A few weeks later, the bunnies who both were males had bitten each other, developed infections, left us and went to bunny heaven. The girls were so upset that we went back to the breeder and the girls picked out one bunny that they named Sport. He lived in a large cage that was transported to Saquish in the Spring and back to Westboro before school started. The girls took great care of him, fed him well and kept his cage clean. With all this affection he had a very long, but simple life. His only activity was when we let him loose in the cottage and he would jump around with Sox and Jake. They were all friends.

One Saturday, after Thanksgiving, we visited Ann's brother Mike and his wife Wanda. Their cat recently had one kitten and Wanda offered it to the girls. Ann knew that I was not fond of cats. When the girls asked her if they could keep it she said, "Ask your Father." I was engrossed in watching a Thanksgiving football game and when asked, not really paying attention, I said, "Yes, if your Mother says its O.K." They immediately ran back to Ann jumping and shouting that Dad said yes. With that, what could Ann say? We left with a new addition to our family.

That night we walked into the kitchen and placed the new arrival on the floor. Jake then walked in, stopped and stared at the new kitten. The kitten then sprang onto the counter and from there to the top of the refrigerator. His fur bristled out like porcupine quills. His back was hunched as he stared at Jake and hissed back. The girls named him Sox because he was a gray tiger with four white feet. As he matured, Sox then went on to establish a reputation at Saquish.

Shortly after that evening, Jake and Sox continued to get acquainted with each other and turned into close buddies. The day the girls finished school in June we would pack everything and head for the beach. One year on the evening we were leaving, our racehorse Jaded Jane was entered in the first race at Lincoln Downs, a horse racing track in Rhode Island. We packed the SUV with the large rabbit cage tied to the top and the rabbit inside in his traveling cage. Jake and Sox always traveled together inside the SUV. We stopped at Lincoln Downs to see the first race, left the three pets in the SUV and lowered the windows. It was a cool evening.

This was the first time our young girls were at a race track and saw their horse run in a race. Jaded Jane, in a photo finish, came in second. They were at first disappointed but learned an important lesson. The lesson learned was that no matter how hard you try you do not always win. Finishing second is not bad.

It is something you can take pride in doing, but you have to try harder the next time. Then we went to the car, where our pets were all luckily being well-behaved, and headed to Saquish for the Summer.

After Jake passed away, for some reason, Sox did not like to travel in the SUV. On Fridays when Ann was packing everything for the weekend, Sox would sense what was coming and would hide in the house. He had three hiding places and when Ann and the girls were ready to go, she would find him in one of those places. They would then drive to Hanover and meet me at the bus stop. Then we would all continue on to the beach.

One Friday Sox was not in any of the three hiding places. For the next two hours Ann, Kathi, Lorri and some neighborhood children all searched in the house, cellar, garage and yard to no avail. Sue Judge our next door neighbor stopped by to see Ann. As they were talking in the kitchen, Sox nonchalantly came walking into the room acting like nothing had happened. Ann had no idea where he was hiding, but never gave him the chance to do it again. Every Friday thereafter, Ann would lock Sox in a room just before she started to pack the car. He could not figure out what was happening nor what day of the week it was, so we had no further problem with Sox hiding.

Once he was in the SUV, he was very upset and uncomfortable. This was the case until we crossed Powder Point Bridge and reached Gurnet Road. Once there he would immediately jump into the front seat and with his back legs on the seat and front legs on the dashboard he would stare straight ahead until we reached the cottage. Evidently it was the bumping of the wheels on the boards of Powder Point Bridge that alerted him to our location.

Sox loved to hunt. Every now and then he would catch a small bunny, mouse or mole. When successful he was proud. He would place it right in front of the cottage door as a gift for Ann. Then he would sit there and proudly wait for Ann to acknowledge it. She would, however, just give him a frown and scold him. With a lowered head, he would walk away. Finally her gifts stopped appearing.

I never was fond of cats. From the day we brought him home I called him Fox, even though he was named by the girls for his four white feet. He was trained as if he were a dog, and he acted that way too. Sox and his personality changed my thinking. I learned why many people consider both cats and dogs as an important part of their family. Sox became one of my close friends. After returning from work and sitting in my recliner he would jump on my lap and make himself comfortable. He would then turn his head and look at me, as if trying to tell me what he had done for the day. By his expressions and actions, I could tell whether he had a good day or a bad day and whether he himself had been good or bad.

If he had a bad day, he would slowly walk back and forth in front of the chair before jumping on my lap. A while later he would turn his head and look at me. If he was bad, he would be nowhere in sight and I would have to go looking for him. After finding him and putting him on my lap, he would not turn his head until I scratched his neck and back and told him everything was O.K. He was as easy to read as a book.

We would often take a walk on the beach with Sandy, Gene and their dog Duke. While we walked on the open sand, Sox walked on the edge of the sand and sea grass sometimes just in the sea grass. He was cautious but brave, and never backed down from any animal. Holding his ground was a priority. Attacking was next. Turning and running was not even a thought.

There was a pathway in the sea grass between our cottage and the Balakier's. On one side the sand was higher and the beach grass thicker than on the other. Their dog Bones would use the pathway to come to our cottage for treats.

Sox would often hide in the high side of the sea grass and wait for Bones to come. When he came by, Sox would jump out and chase him down the path. It happened enough times that from the porch you could see the process developing and if you waited, sure enough it would happen. Bones liked the treats more than the concern with a cat chasing him. He never stopped coming for treats, at approximately the same time every afternoon, and Sox never stopped hiding and chasing him. They never fought or had territorial disputes. Evidently for Sox it was just a game that he enjoyed. It might have been the same for Bones.

One time after midnight we heard some loud barking and screeching coming from the Balakier's porch. Two large dogs had Sox pinned on top of a rail pole. They were trying to jump up and grab him and he was defending himself with his claws. As I came onto the porch, Richard was already there yelling at the dogs. Without help would Sox have survived a fight with two large vicious dogs? It's unlikely, but I wouldn't bet against him. When needed, his claws were sharp and swift.

When Danny and Sandy Keegan bought the cottage next to us it was in the early Fall. We left and went home, not to return until Spring. They had a large Bullmastiff dog named Casey. She weighed well over 100 pounds and had a neck as thick as her head. They came to Saquish all Winter and Casey had the run of the beach. Until the following Spring, she was the only animal there and thought she owned the beach.

When we first went to Saquish the next Spring, Sox was with us. When he went onto the front porch, Casey saw him and thought that an intruder had trespassed on her territory. She stared at Sox then rambled across the sand to our front steps. Sox sat on top of the steps with one paw raised in the air.

Casey started up the steps then stopped two steps from the top. She took one more step and Sox's paw came down like lightning with a claw going deep into Casey's nose. The blood gushed out like it was a newfound oil well. Casey yelped all the way back to her porch. Thankfully Sox did not go for her eye.

That evening Ann and I went to the Keegan's for dinner. Sox came with us and sat outside on the front porch, right in front of the steps. Casey was on the beach and wanted to come into the cottage, but she did not attempt to climb the steps with Sox sitting there. She roamed back and forth in front. Finally she went to the back of the cottage, climbed the steps and came to the back door. Sox and Casey became friends and never had another confrontation. They were not close, but respected each other.

When Sox passed away he was seventeen years old. We were near retirement and decided the time for pets was over. Casey then became very close to us. She in effect became our rent-a-pet and stayed with us for a number of nights at a time after Sandy and Danny went back to Hanover for the week. When you talked to her, she would look right at your eyes. This created a feeling that she understood every word you said. Sox was the most intelligent cat and Casey the most intelligent dog I had ever known. She had a very large body and an easy-going, pleasant disposition. Her size frightened many people, particularly hunters who came near the cottage in the Fall.

Casey had three unique characteristics. She was often challenged on the beach by other dogs, some large and some small. When one tried to attack, she would hold her ground. Her head would then bend down under the dog and with her strength, she would flip it onto its side. Then she would pin the dog down with her large mouth around its neck and the dog would just freeze. After a short while Casey would step back, the dog would stand up and take off down the beach, with its tail between its legs. For some reason Casey never hurt or cut a dog after she pinned it down. She also never lost another confrontation after her first one with Sox, except for her only confrontation with a skunk.

The second characteristic was her reaction to the word "cookie." If you said cookie a few times she would drool. If you said it a number of times, large drools would creep down and hang from her jowls. This is a Bullmastiff characteristic.

Boat people would quite often have a picnic on the beach and leave the cans, bottles and rubbish there. If Sandy saw any people that didn't belong, sitting down on a blanket, and they looked suspicious she would call Casey. Then Sandy would say, "Cookie Casey Cookie." After repeating it a few times Casey looked like a large vicious animal with rabies. Sandy would then point toward the beach and repeat the words.

Casey would amble down to the blanket and slowly circle it a couple of times. She would then nonchalantly sit on the edge of the blanket waiting for a cookie. The panicked people would then pick up their belongings and carefully move on. There is nothing like a large animal looking like it has rabies to ruin a good beach picnic.

Her third characteristic was an attraction to large rocks. During low tides Casey would roam the beach until she found a 3-5 pound rock protruding from the sand. She would dig it out with her two front paws, throwing the sand back between her hind legs. Once loose she would push it up and down the beach with her nose. When she finished blood would often drip from scrapes in her large nose. Don't know what fun or pleasure she achieved from doing it, but she really enjoyed it, bloody nose and all.

When Casey passed away, Sandy obtained a beautiful looking Golden Lab named Bailey. He had a pleasant disposition and liked to run marathons. He would run from The Gurnet Road near Powder Point Bridge all the way to their cottage. Our granddaughter Sydney loved him.

However, as good as Bailey was, no dog could ever replace Casey.

CHAPTER 15

WILDLIFE

Saquish has a large number of different creatures that frequent the peninsula. Some are very common and are seen daily. Others are seldom seen and often only once by a small number of people. My intent is not to discuss every one that was there or was seen there, but to touch on many of the more common and cover the rare and unique ones, including some of the quaint experiences that they provided us.

BIRDS

There are three types of seagulls that consistently frequent Saquish. They are the Herring Gull which is the biggest and has black wing tips. The Ring Billed Gull, which is smaller but seen more often than the Herring. The third is the Laughing Gull which is the most common of the three. For the last two, their names describe their dominant characteristic. Still other gulls are often seen from time to time.

There are also a number of terns, sandpipers and plovers that frequent our beach and the road to The Gurnet. The most famous or infamous of which is the Piping Plover. These are presumed to be so important that vehicles are required to travel a maximum of 5 MPH through areas where they are nesting. Contrast this with 15 MPH to protect our children in school zones.

Cormorants, a voracious diving bird with a long neck and hooked bill, frequented the rocks near The Gurnet. They dive, grab a fish with its bill, surface and with one gulp swallow the whole fish, head first. I have seen one swallow a fish that was over 14" long, when I was fishing for sea trout in Florida. We had just released one, after measuring it that was a little too short to keep. A cormorant dove after it, came up with the trout in its mouth and with one gulp it was gone. In Asia they are used to harvest fish. A metal ring is placed around their neck which prevents them from swallowing the fish. A small line is tied to the cormorant which the fishermen use to manually retrieve the bird and remove the fish from its mouth.

In the Summer, our marshes are home to Great Blue Herons which are mainly grey in color and Great Egrets, which are pure white. Both birds have long darkish-yellow pointed bills. These are large wading birds that have migrated from the South to spend the Summers here and enjoy it with us. Every now and then an Osprey is spotted. They have not yet started to consistently nest in our marshes, but have in Kingston Bay.

Ducks are becoming increasingly common, with Mallards the predominant type. On a recent spring day I saw six Canada Geese on the beach. As common as they are inland, these were the only ones seen at Saquish.

One fall afternoon as Ann and I sat in our observation room, a large flock of Snow Geese flew past the windows. They made two trips back and forth across the beach. You guessed it, all their feathers were colored as white as snow. On their trip South, that night was spent nestled into the cove at Western Point. Don't know how comfortable it was, but doubt it equaled the motel comfort of our trips South.

In the Fall, Barn Swallows prepare for their migration. Flocks of hundreds, if not thousands fly randomly in mass from one landing area to another amongst the cottages. At times they are so thick that it is hard to see through the flock. This lasts for more than two weeks and then they are gone. We don't know whether they make it in one continuous flight or stop for a night or two. In either case, like a sport team preparing for its upcoming season, they are well prepared and strengthened for their upcoming journey.

While sitting in the observation room watching the Barn Swallows, a hawk was often seen. They were different types and would glide over the grassy covered sand dunes looking for mice, moles or anything else that was edible. At times they glided close enough to almost touch.

One time while driving from the bridge to The Gurnet, there was a beautifully colored Cock Pheasant that crossed the road in front of me. A strange place for that type of bird.

For years there were Wild Turkeys on the mainland. We have seen them on the local golf courses and on the Duxbury streets. In our last summer at Saquish, we finally saw one on the peninsula. On a Saturday evening the Deans and Keagans were going with us into town for dinner. As we started up the incline to The Gurnet, a Wild Turkey hen was standing in the middle of the road. We stopped and watched it slowly walk into the bushes. Just another example of a local from the mainland finding and enjoying the amenities of Saquish and The Gurnet.

Every now and then the birdwatchers network would report a rare or very rare bird seen at Saquish. Once I met a man who was walking near the curve with a backpack and camera and said he came from California. He had received word of a rare European bird that was sighted at Saquish Beach. He wanted to add its name to his list of sightings. I don't know how successful he was and don't recall the bird's name. If successful, it was a lot less expensive and easier than flying to Europe from both a financial and distance perspective. If not, he could always fly to Europe later.

Just about every Winter, Snowy Owls would migrate from the Arctic. Some would settle at Logan Airport in Boston, where they were trapped and then often released on our peninsula. Their heads were large and bodies were white as snow. Young birds and females had short black horizontal bars interspersed across their heads and bodies. While they perched on a fence pole or were standing in the marsh, they looked majestic. When you stopped to watch one, it could put you in a semi-hypnotic state.

We often spent New Years Eves with Sandy and Danny at their cottage. One year we walked to The Gurnet to attend a New Year's Eve celebration. We left the party at one o'clock in the morning and walked back under a bright full moon. As we reached the beach, there was a large pure white Snowy Owl perched on a fence pole in front of us. As we came close, it would fly further down the beach, perch on another pole and wait for us. The owl repeated this procedure a number of times. With the full moon brightening the beach, and the Snowy Owl interacting with us, all on a New Year's Eve, this was a once in a lifetime experience.

ANIMALS

Mice, moles and voles have always lived in the sand dunes and thick undergrowth near the beach. Although they are food for many other species, their numbers seem to stay constant.

After Dad retired, he and Mom would spend a number of weeks each year living at the cottage. Dad was an experienced fisherman, hunter and trapper. He bought himself a trap that would catch small animals alive. His intent was to catch and remove the varmints. He also hoped to catch a wild rabbit or two to eat. He caught a fair amount of rodents, no rabbits but did trap two opossums. This was before the Blizzard of '78 which flooded a major part of the peninsula. After that we never saw another opossum.

During the early years, skunks were prevalent. There was a family that had a home under Goose and Marge's cottage which was next to ours. One evening, I saw two skunks go under Goose's small shed. When I told Goose, he said that getting rid of them was no problem. Ex-lax was put near the entrance to the nest so the skunks would eat it. They then would mess in the nest and abandon it. This worked.

One evening Ann and I took a walk to Bennet's Point. The entrance to it was a narrow strip of land, about twelve feet wide when the tide was high, with the bay on both sides. At night we always had a flashlight with us. As we were returning, two skunks were coming right at us. We froze! The skunks froze!

There was no question who was going to move first. We back peddled. The skunks stayed frozen looking right at us. They won as we walked back to Bennet's Point. One half hour later we cautiously walked off the narrow strip. We don't know if the skunks saw us, but we didn't see them. That ended our romantic evening.

Our cat Sox, who was afraid of no animal, was sprayed three times by a skunk. We would wash him with tomato juice in the deep kitchen sink. He detested this and would cry and screech. After three times either the skunk smell, the tomato juice wash or a combination of both had taught him a lesson.

Sandy and Danny's dog Casey was sprayed once, right in the face. She had to stay outside for a couple of days until the smell disappeared. Casey unlike Sox was a fast learner.

Clark's Island, although a part of Plymouth, is located in Duxbury Bay, just to the Northwest of Western Point, and is separated from it by a water channel. There was a sea gull rockery on the island and a house was built close to it. The gulls adopted the house as a place to perch for the night. If you know what a few sea gulls can do to a boat, imagine what one hundred or more can do to a house. Somehow a number of Red Fox showed up on the island. Some of the fox then migrated across the channel to Saquish. Jean Cotti-Johnson found a nest of young ones under her cottage. The foxes didn't last long at Saquish, but every now and then somebody would see one, which might have been purposely relocated from the mainland.

Initially deer were seldom seen. Over the years their numbers have increased a great deal. A decent amount of them have made Clark's Island their home and every now and then they were seen swimming across the bay from Duxbury. For a couple of years a family of deer have wintered amongst the cottages on Western Point and are often seen near the beach. In the Summer, deer tracks are seen on the sandy cart paths behind our cottage.

One morning, two adults and a fawn were seen eating the bulbs on Ann's Yucca plants, just before they were ready to bloom. A few mornings later the deer jumped over a fence and raided a garden two lots away from ours. From then on, deer repellant packages were suspended near our garden and plants. Let them go somewhere else for breakfast.

When we built our cottage, wild rabbits were everywhere on the whole peninsula. If you drove to the beach in the early evening, it was common to see a couple of them on the gravel road between High Pines and The Gurnet. In driving the short distance across The Gurnet, you often would see five or six rabbits munching on the lawns. When we reached our cottage, we might see one or two more in the grassy sand dunes or near our garden. There were nearly as many rabbits as there were mice or moles.

Nothing bothered them except a few hunters with beagles in the Fall.

One year a coyote found the peninsula and established a nest at High Pines. Shortly thereafter it was joined by a second coyote. The rabbit population started to diminish. When six coyote pups showed up, the rabbit population was just about eliminated. When this happened, the coyote population would follow the trend and decreased. This counterbalancing of rabbit and coyote populations has continued.

Sometimes during a full moon, you could hear the coyotes howl. Even though you could hear more than one howl, other than the time that we saw the mother and her pups, we only saw one of them at a time. At dusk or during the evening, you might see one prowling the road to The Gurnet, the beach or marsh and even the shoreline at Clark's Island. Their food was mainly small animals so they didn't hunt in packs. To my knowledge, they never caused any problems with people or their pets.

Over the last few years some residents have reported seeing a Fisher Cat near the thick vegetation before Western Point. If true, it would be the rarest of all four-legged animals seen on the peninsula.

MARINE MAMMALS

The most common marine mammal at Saquish is the seal. Initially they would arrive in the Fall and stay all Winter. A group of them would congregate around the rocks at The Gurnet. When you went there to fish for stripers, if the seals were there, the stripers weren't.

In winter days when we walked the beach, a seal would often follow us. It would be swimming parallel to the way you were walking. Its black head would pop up out of the ocean, take a look at you and go back down. This would continue for a good part of our walk on the then vacant beach.

It was uncommon to see a seal in the Summer. Many years ago, however, my mother and Ann were walking the beach on a dark evening. A large seal was lying near the beach grass above the high tide level. They didn't notice it and just before reaching the seal, it scrambled down the beach and headed for the water. Scared the hell out of Mom and Ann.

We never again saw a live seal on the beach again until a couple of years ago. Before leaving for Florida, Ann and I were collecting dry beach grass to cover the sand dunes. We saw a baby seal, a little over three feet long on the beach near low tide. The tracks showed it had followed the outgoing tide to the waters edge. As I walked near, it lifted its head and barked at me while snapping its jaws.

We thought it was hurt so Ann called the Plymouth Harbor Master to report it. A few minutes later he called back and said he contacted a local organization that administered to marine mammals. In about an hour they would arrive at Saquish and contact us. A plan of action would follow. After arriving and visually checking it, they determined it was a Gray Seal pup that leaves its mother soon after birth and appeared O.K. It was just tired and might stay on the beach for a couple of days to regain its strength. They asked us to watch it and let them know if anything changed.

Late that afternoon as the tide was working its way in, the seal was working its way up the beach staying ahead of the tide. In the evening, after the tide had receded, we went back with flashlights to check and found it was gone. There were no tracks in the sand to indicate it had followed the outgoing tide. The next morning there were no signs of it anywhere. It must have just slipped into the ocean at high tide and swam away.

There were two times when whales had visited the area. One was a baby whale that was staying near the Bell out beyond The Gurnet. This was the first marker into Plymouth Harbor and a sounding signal to make you aware of the rocks around The Gurnet. You could easily reach it with a small motorboat, pull alongside the small whale and pet it. Some people speculated that the baby had lost its mother and adopted the Bell with its noise as a surrogate. One day late in the Summer, it was no longer at the Bell and was never seen again.

Very late on a Saturday evening in July 1979, a young Pilot Whale washed up on the beach at the curve. A number of the younger people who were partying there initially thought it was a shark, but then realized it was a whale. They turned on the lights in their jeeps, blew their horns and did everything they could to scare it back. This included rolling up their pant legs, wading in the water and trying to push it out with the receding tide. The whale was 15 feet long and weighed about 2000 pounds. Unfortunately their efforts were unsuccessful.

Early the next morning approximately 75 people had congregated at the curve. They had brought beach umbrellas, buckets, pails, bed sheets and quickly became well organized. The bed sheets and beach umbrellas were used to cover the whale. This lessened the impact from the burning sun.

By this time the tide had receded a considerable distance. A long line of people were stationed from the whale to the water. Five-gallon buckets were consecutively filled, passed up the line and poured over the sheets and the whale. After a number of buckets were emptied, they were stacked and returned to the water. The process continued at a steady pace for the rest of the morning. The Aquarium in Boston was contacted and they promised to send a special hoist, stretcher and large tank to take the whale back to their location in Boston. We were advised to keep pouring water on the whale until they arrived around noon or later, and we did.

When you approached the whale, her big eye looked right at you. Her expression told you that she knew we were trying to help. Every now and then, after buckets of water were poured over her, she would pleasantly moan, as if trying to thank you. When the Aquarium staff arrived they took blood samples, hoisted her into a tank on their truck and went back to Boston.

The Boston, Plymouth and Middlesex newspapers along with the Associated Press had articles about her rescue and status. The evening news on the Boston T.V. stations ran highlights about her. She was the healthiest of any whale to come under the Aquarium's care. The people at Saquish were given a great deal of credit for preventing any major problems that might have resulted from heat exhaustion. The newspapers, T.V. and the public affectionately gave her the name "SAQUISH."

She stayed at the Aquarium where she was cared for, and then a few days later she was transported from the Aquarium back to her home. She was released over thirty miles from Boston, out beyond Provincetown, where the water was over 100′ deep. There were a number of Finback and Humpback Whales in the area, which indicated a good food supply was available.

Even though wildlife professionals tried to track her movements, she quickly disappeared. One of the principals involved in the release was asked why there were not more sightings of her in the open ocean. To that question he replied:

"It's a mighty big ocean and a mighty little whale."

CHAPTER 16

NATURE

Nature, by its very nature mimics the saying "The Good, The Bad and The Ugly." At Saquish you experienced many of nature's characteristics, ranging from the beautiful to the turbulent.

In the morning you could watch the sun as it rose out of the ocean and then as it set at dusk over the Back Bay. On a full moon you could do the same. The Harvest Moon was always a large brilliant orange-yellowish color that would glow as it emerged from the ocean.

Every now and then, after a thunderstorm, a bright, thick double rainbow would appear and cover a full 180 degree span. It would start in the ocean, go over The Gurnet and Front Bay then would disappear into the Pine Hills of Plymouth.

In the Fall as you sat in the observation room you could see flocks of Barn Swallows and other birds that were migrating South for the Winter. There were hawks gliding back and forth over the beach grass looking for anything they could catch and eat.

On the hot, humid summer days, where the humidity was high on the mainland, it was much lower at Saquish since it was surrounded by cool water. At night you could breathe the clean, fresh ocean air. It was not infested with pollutants often found in the cities and towns. No one at Saquish had air conditioning. Over the forty Summers we lived there, you could count the hot uncomfortable nights on one hand. The environment was so good that a few days of rain was a real inconvenience. Major storms, although few over the forty year period, were occurrences you remembered the most.

The first hurricane was at the end of our initial Summer on Labor Day weekend and is discussed in Chapter 4. This one was the severest of all. Just before the next two, we left and took the girls back to Westboro. During one of these storms, my mother and father stayed at the beach. During the height of the storm they went to the high ground at The Gurnet Lighthouse and rode it out in their SUV.

When Cory was two months old, Lorri brought him to Saquish for a week of vacation. During that week a hurricane came through the area. We went to Hanover and stayed at Sandy and Danny's home for the night.

The hurricane decreased in intensity before it blew through and had no effect. There were a number of other hurricane threats that either dissipated or moved out to sea before they reached the beach.

Hurricanes did little damage to the beach, but the pre-hurricane hype had an emotional effect on the cottage owners. These storms did, however, raise havoc with motorboats. The heavy rains and large swells would cause some boats to sink. Mooring ropes would then either break or pull the mooring loose from the ocean bed. The boats were then either smashed against the rocks, sank, drifted out to sea or were washed up onto the beach. This type of storm passed through in a matter of hours. Some impact would last for a few high tides, but would decrease in intensity with each additional one. There were no large trees or telephone poles, since there was no commercial electric or telephone service. Some of the dunes would wash away, but nothing of a major affect.

The real damage to the beach came on nor'easters that accompanied a high tide. They lasted for two or more days. On an extremely high moon tide, the swing from low to high was over 14' on the vertical. The time from low to high is just over six hours. By comparison, when the moon is in the third quarter, the swing is less than 7' on the vertical. During the peak of a nor'easter, the waves could extend more than 12' above normal. On the two major storms described next, the tide did not recede from high to low for a few days.

In February of 1978, there was a major nor'easter with extensive winds that lasted for a few days. It became known as the Blizzard of '78. Duxbury Beach was devastated with a number of breakthroughs from the main ocean to the Back Bay. This prohibited any form of ground transportation from reaching The Gurnet or Saquish. There was some misinformation that Saquish was completely underwater. We finally received word from the Harbor Master that except for a few cottages, Saquish had withstood the storm. It took over a week for the Army Corps of Engineers, using military type heavy duty equipment, to repair the break throughs at Duxbury Beach.

We were then able to drive to Saquish. The sand dunes looked like someone had taken a cake knife, gone back twenty feet, and vertically sliced them off. No damage was done to our or our next door neighbors' cottages.

From then on, we no longer drove from the beach to the front of our cottage to park our SUV, but instead parked it behind the cottage. The front was only used for foot traffic. Snow fences and dry beach grass were used in the Fall to cover, protect and help build the sand dunes in the front. Over the next few years, this helped them gain back what was lost in the major storm.

The Summer before the Blizzard of '78, I sold our 12' boat and bought a new 14' aluminum boat with a trailer and twenty-five horsepower motor. The 12' boat was always towed on a skid to the front of the cottage, tied down and left there for the Winter. This was not feasible with a larger boat and trailer. Stanley Bien, whose cottage was four lots away let us store the boat and trailer underneath his cottage. The cottage was level with the beach and every Winter, water would flow up close to the cottage. However, to our knowledge, it had never gone underneath. The Blizzard pulverized our boat, and trailer. They were continually smashed back and forth against the cottage pilings with no way out. The cottage survived with little damage. From then on, our boat and trailer were stored behind our cottage for the Winter.

After the blizzard, the weather was rather peaceful until 1991. Then the No Name Storm AKA "The Perfect Storm" battered both Duxbury and Saquish Beach with much greater force than the Blizzard of '78.

Duxbury immediately contacted the Army Corps of Engineers who responded and repaired the multitude of breakthroughs and blow-throughs on Duxbury Beach. Again there was no vehicular traffic allowed through Duxbury Beach for over a week. The initial report from the Harbor Master was much worse than that of the Blizzard of '78. The sand dunes were devastated and a few more cottages were knocked down and demolished.

On Saturday, over a week later, owners of property on Saquish were allowed to come to the Duxbury Beach parking lot and climb onto the back of a pickup truck. You were then transported to Saquish. The Corp of Engineers was still working and every now and then you stopped to let a large piece of equipment go by. Duxbury Beach looked like it was hit with a number of bombs. There was no vegetation left, just sand and gravel for miles. It was as flat as a pancake. It appeared someone had waved a magic wand over the rose bushes, thick vegetation and high sand dunes and they had just disappeared from sight. You had two hours at the beach to check your property, then leave by way of the pickup truck.

Danny and I were on one of the first pickups trips, Ann and Sandy came on a later one. They were sitting in the cargo area when the truck had to stop. Ann stood up to video the devastated area. Suddenly the driver gunned the truck and Ann fell out over the back tailgate. She landed in soft sand and luckily did not get hurt. The truck stopped, Ann climbed back on, she brushed off the sand and they continued to Saquish.

The sand dune in front of our cottage had washed out up to twenty feet from the front steps. Again it looked like a cake knife was used to cut the dune, this time to a 10' to 12' vertical drop. As the waves smashed against the sand dunes tearing them down, they also jumped up over the dunes and crashed right at my steps. This created a four-foot wide by three-foot deep trench. It started in front of the steps, went underneath the cottage and ended up at the shed in back.

The steps were still attached to the cottage, but were hanging suspended. Nothing else but the large galvanized bolts, that we had obtained when we were collecting the telephone poles, kept them attached to the porch and stopped them from being torn away. The boat trailer in back of the shed was buried in sand. Thankfully the motor was secure in the shed. The boat sat on top of the sand with the trailer buried beneath it. The boat was still attached to the winch which was the only part of the trailer showing. Later we had to dig out the front end and jack it up. It was then attached to the hitch on the SUV and pulled free. This was quite an effort. After seeing the devastation the first thing we did was to retrieve a 15′ ladder and place it against the vertical sand dune. Ann and Sandy used it to climb from the beach to the top of the dune, when they arrived.

Danny kept his boat on the front side of his cottage for the Winter. The sand dune sloped from the front of the cottage to the back where there was a cellar. The waves lifted the boat off the trailer, smashed it against the supporting cottage poles as it worked its way to the back and deposited the remaining pieces in back of the cottage. The cellar was filled with over two feet of sand. It was a backbreaking effort to remove the sand by hand with a wheelbarrow.

Ann and Sandy checked the inside of the cottages which, were O.K. and then walked the beach to check the devastation up close. It was a mess! After two hours, we climbed back into the truck, with the knowledge that both cottages were in good shape. There was substantial sand dune and beach work to do in the Spring, but it could wait until then. That Spring, Danny and I dug a four-foot deep trench and ran a row of eight foot high chain link fence in front of the cottage. Four feet was buried in the ground, and four feet was left above. It helped to build up the sand dunes and stopped the minor storms from taking the sand away, but over the next fifteen years nor'easters of a much lesser intensity destroyed the fence piece by piece.

Initially after a major storm you could hire someone with a front-end loader to move sand from the lower beach. This would help rebuild the sand dunes. This is no longer allowed by Plymouth. Snow fence and dry marsh grass are two of the best resources to rebuild the dunes. Since 1991 there were a number of nor'easters, but nowhere near as intense as the Blizzard of '78 or the No Name Storm of '91 One Summer, however, a storm with strong winds and heavy rains hit us. It lasted a couple of days. My boat was on a mooring in front of the cottage. That Saturday afternoon someone saw it break loose and head toward Plymouth. Even with the rough surf, Richard Balakier and I, with Richard's insistence, were able to launch his boat and head toward Plymouth Bay and Kingston Bay to search for it. With the high waves, the going was rough and our visibility was very limited.

After a short time we dejectedly returned to the beach.

A week later the Plymouth Harbor Master called me. My boat was found, beached near Burt's Restaurant, diagonally across the bay from our cottage. We went to retrieve it with the boat trailer. To our surprise, both the boat, and motor were thrown against the many large rocks that lined the beach. Both were torn to pieces. They were left there for disposal by the Harbor Master. Hope the price of aluminum was high at that time.

The one attribute of nature that we feared the most was fire. It takes a fair amount of time to reach Saquish from Duxbury or Marshfield and much longer from Plymouth, although the fire departments respond as soon as possible considering the condition of the road, cart paths and tides. Lightning storms are very common with large bolts of lightning quickly followed by loud roaring thunder. Every time one exploded near you, you would shudder with fear and quickly lower your head, as if subconsciously trying to get out of the way. Other storms are less intense but have hundreds of short streaks of lightning taking place at the same time, a sight to experience.

Over the forty years, there were a few cottages that were struck by lightning. There are two instances that were the most vivid. The first was at Western Point. The owners had left that afternoon and lightning struck the cottage late that evening. No one was nearby to notice what had happened. As the fire spread, the 100 pound natural gas bottles, that were used for fuel, caught fire and exploded. Before the fire departments arrived the cottage burnt to the ground. The owners received permits from Plymouth and completely rebuilt the cottage.

The second happened during a late afternoon thunderstorm. A cottage close to ours was hit by lightning and caught fire. It was rented at the time and there were a number of people in it and the surrounding cottages. Two of our residents had spent their careers as firefighters. Their quick knowledgeable response, coupled with support from others was able to contain and put out the fire with minimal damage.

For years Ann used a Laundromat in Green Harbor and knew the people that worked there. An older person who lived on The Gurnet worked the nightshift. One evening, after returning from Boston where she was visiting our daughter Kathi, Ann came across a car that was stopped on the dirt road leading to The Gurnet. It belonged to the older fellow who had just closed the Laundromat. His car had stopped and would not start. Ann gave him a push with our car. His car started, went as far as The Gurnet then stopped again. She gave him a second push. His car started again, and she followed him home. He parked his car very close to his house, thanked Ann and went in to join his wife.

As Ann was leaving she happened to look in the back mirror and noticed that the car had started on fire. She backed up, took out a few gallons of recently bought water and tried to put out the fire. This was not successful. She then banged on the house door and yelled as loud as she could but there was no response. Eric Nudd who lived nearby heard Ann yelling and came running with a fire extinguisher. He was able to quench the flames. A near catastrophe averted.

There were two vehicles that completely burned on Saquish. The granddaughter of a Saquish resident had driven off the beach. On her return she took the back road, which in places was only wide enough for one vehicle to pass. The vehicle exiting the beach always had the right of way. When she met a leaving vehicle she drove onto the soft sand which had a fair amount of dry beach grass on it. Inexperienced, she buried the vehicle in the sand, but still tried to get out. The hot catalytic converter ignited the beach grass. The vehicle then burst into flames, with huge clouds of black smoke rising into the air. No one was hurt but nothing was left of the vehicle.

One year Pat and Eddie Billington, who were Ann's childhood friends, were visiting us for the weekend. Shortly after midnight, Ann heard a car horn blowing. She jumped out of bed and ran into Pat and Eddie, who had seen flames from their bedroom window. All three ran up the stairs to get a better look from our observation room. It was very dark but they could see roaring flames about five lots away. Ann thought it was either the Tilden's or Cotti's cottage, and immediately called the Duxbury Fire Department. They said they had already received two calls and the fire truck was on its way. She then called Marty Bosworth a former fire chief who headed up our de facto Saquish Fire Department.

A vehicle in a vacant lot located right next to a right of way had somehow caught on fire. A number of residents had started to fight the fire using fire extinguishers. This stopped it from spreading into the nearby bushes and causing more damage. Marty soon arrived and took control. With the fire extinguishers that people had brought, coupled with shovels to throw on sand and a water hose that was connected to Tilden's water tank, the fire was soon extinguished. The fire trucks from Duxbury and Plymouth then arrived. They arrived too late to help, but the fact they responded quickly, which they always did, was appreciated. Kudos to our own de facto fire department.

Powder Point Bridge, a wooden bridge, was our major access to Saquish. It went across the bay from Duxbury to Duxbury Beach. In 1985 a fire, started one night by a fisherman's lantern, damaged 200 feet of the bridge. When the state inspected the bridge they also found weaknesses in other areas. In July the bridge was officially closed. It took two years to replace the old bridge with a new wooden bridge. It was reopened in August 1987. During those two years, our only access was through Marshfield and the Duxbury Beach parking lots.

There are times when nature is very deceiving. Picture yourself in the following scenario. You have just bought a brand new 4- wheel drive SUV and want to test it out and show it off. You invite your best friend to spend the day with you and your new vehicle. He or she has spent a day at Saquish in the past and suggests you go there to test it out. Neither of you are familiar with tidal conditions.

You drive The Gurnet Road, cross over The Gurnet, pass through the lowland area traverse the sand dunes and approach the beach. To the left you see open beach and sand bars that stretch for a few hundred yards. There are no vehicles there so you decide to spend some time on the sand bar closest to the open ocean. It is not a straight drive to the sand bar. There are a number of small dry trenches over two feet deep. They were created by the water rushing in and draining out. Now, however they are dry so you skirt around them and reach your destination.

It is a calm, warm sunny day. A beautiful day to spend at the beach. You decide to either lay in the sun and get a tan or stay in the car. To take a nap or play a game, it's your choice. In either case you lose track of what's happening, especially with the tide. Unbeknown to you, this is the time of a full moon. In the six hours, from low to high, the tide will rise 14' on the vertical. You happened to arrive right at the time the tide had just reached its low point. It would soon turn and start to flow in rapidly gaining momentum and height.

A while later, you look out and are shocked to see the water has surrounded the sand bar and you snap to attention. It is rising at a good rate and your only thought is to get back to dry land. Panic sets in and you drive in a straight line for the main beach, forgetting about the trenches that were skirted on the way out. The vehicle hits a trench, stops, bogs down in the water, gets stuck in the sand and does not move. Water is seeping up through the floorboards. There is no way to get help for the vehicle so very reluctantly, yet quickly, you abandon it and wade to shore. Then you watch as your life's dream slowly disappears into the rising ocean. Ten hours later a tow truck will haul the vehicle off the sand bar and back to the mainland. During the forty years at Saquish we saw or heard of a similar scenario a number of times. This didn't happen to just inexperienced people. Others that knew better just pushed their luck too far.

To you the day was a disaster. To many others it was just another calm, warm sunny day. A beautiful day to spend at the beach.

CHAPTER 17

THE GURNET - SAQUISH ASSOCIATION

The Gurnet-Saquish Association was formed under Massachusetts General Laws, Chapter 180 with Hank Cahill as President on July 26, 1970. Its purpose is contained in a page and a half of legalese. In layman's language, it is to promote both conservation and the interest of its residents while working with the towns of Plymouth and Duxbury. Membership is optional but, in general, requires that you own a livable building on the peninsula. Ann and I joined the organization in 1971, when we spent our first Summer there. Shortly thereafter I was elected to the Board of Directors.

Initially a major focus of the board was on conservation related issues. These included mainly the planting and fertilization of beach grass, the constructing of snow fences and road repairs. A second focus was on activities for the children. On Thursday mornings the association arranged for an instructor to teach arts and crafts or give swimming lessons to the children who were at the beach. Our girls enjoyed everything except for being in the cold water.

As we moved into the late seventies and four-wheel drives became more common, many nonresidents started to use our private beach and vandalism increased. One Saturday evening a number of items were stolen from boats that were on trailers and from property that was on the front beach. The next morning a Board of Directors meeting was held and it was decided to have volunteers man a gate at the entrance to The Gurnet. They would stop all nonresidents and uninvited guests from entering, since the right of ways and the beach were private.

During Friday evenings, all day Saturday, Saturday evenings and all day Sunday teams of two volunteers would take shifts staffing the gate. This became known as "Gate Watch." It caused much consternation and aggravation with the town of Plymouth and a number of its residents, resulting in their acquiring legal opinions regarding this matter. The results confirmed that the access roads and beach were private, but did not define who owned them. Plymouth owned land at Saquish but their residents did not have the right to use it unless the town gave them permission. This was the same as other buildings and property owned by the town. Plymouth elected not to grant permission due to other concerns like bathroom facilities, parking and accessing private property during high tides.

Late one Saturday evening when Ann and I were on Gate Watch duty, from eight o'clock until midnight, the night was very dark yet clear. There was hardly any traffic during the whole watch. All of a sudden we saw a large light in the sky over the ocean near Powder Point Bridge. The light came towards us and then stopped and stayed stationary. This continued for a number of times. We thought about a helicopter, but could not hear any noise. This was about the time that discussions of flying saucers were common. We talked about the potential implications of this, and on a dark night with no one around you acquired a very eerie feeling. Finally as it came closer and passed by us we could hear sounds that indicated it was a helicopter, but a very quiet one.

By the summer of 1981, the organization was effective but loosely run. There was no list of members, just the amount of money collected. Fundraising amounted to one raffle a year. A grill was bought for around $100. Tickets were sold for 25¢ apiece. The profits ranged from $150 to $200. A lot of work for a small return.

The Blizzard of '78 had substantially increased our cost of conservation. The residents were getting tired of volunteering for Gate Watch, even though it was a necessity. Committees were appointed as needed. At Directors Meetings we often discussed items from one meeting to the next, with no action taken unless it was an absolute necessity.

One Summer I was approached by the nominating committee and told that neither of our two vice-presidents were able to take the position of President for the next year. They asked me to take that responsibility. After much consideration, I agreed provided they bought into a plan we should implement. They listened and wholeheartedly agreed.

The plan would take two years for full implementation. At that time the President's term was one year, so the First Vice-president would have to buy in and continue to implement the plan the following year, when he or she became President. Ken McNair, a very close friend, who owned his own business and would call a spade a spade, was our man. I had talked to Ken about this and he had bought in if he was asked to take the First Vice-president position.

Four full-time committees were established. Two would raise revenue. They were Membership and Fundraising. Two would spend it. They were Conservation and Security. The name "Gate Watch" was so prevalent however that it prevailed and Security was less frequently used. A chairperson was appointed to head up each committee and recruit members. Their committee plans were then brought to the Directors Meetings for discussion and a decision. The only other expenses were minor administrative costs to run the organization.

During my term the plan was put into place. During Ken's term the plan was fully implemented. We immediately appointed four committee chairpersons and hired a Saquish resident to handle Gate Watch duty. Membership lists were established and the committee recruited new members. Conservation continued to do an excellent job, but due to nature and increased resident use of the right of ways, it required additional funding. Over time fundraising was a big success. Ken loved to play horseshoes and a fund raiser, the "Annual Ken McNair Horseshoe Tournament," was established in his memory.

In the mid eighties, Ann joined the board and took an active role in fundraising. Her first recommendation was to buy 200 beach towels with a Saquish logo and sell them to residents and friends. The association's cost was $4 per towel and the selling price would be $8. This provided a 100% profit since there were no additional expenses. Some of the board members were against the idea. They were concerned that we would lose money and end up owning a host of beach towels. Since none of them went swimming, they had no use for beach towels. Ann was very persistent and was given approval. All 200 towels were sold by Memorial Day. She bought 200 more and by July 4th there were only twenty five towels left.

In 1976, most cities and towns had parades to celebrate our country's Bicentennial Anniversary. Not wanting to be left out, Carolyn Poirier established a 4th of July parade for the Gurnet- Saquish residents. The parade was such a success that it is held every year, with the same amount of participation that we had in 1976 Prior to one of the 4th of July parades, Ann bought four towels which she made into two robes along with signs advertising the towels for sale. She also made crowns representing a Queen and King. Wearing the robes with the crowns and carrying the signs we marched in the parade

THE FOURTH OF JULY PARADE

Ann's sign read
THE QUEEN
WANTS THIS
TO BE A WHALE
OF A DAY
BUY YOUR
TOWEL FROM
HER TODAY!

My sign said
FUND RAISER
BEACH TOWELS
$8
SUPPORT
GURNET
SAQUISH ASSOC.

We carried the for sale towels in our hands and before the parade was over, all the towels were sold.

A $1600 profit was very substantial for that time. Over the next number of years, the beach towel sale was repeated three times. Shortly after the towel success, Ann suggested that we change the raffle. Instead of buying a grill and selling chances for 25¢ apiece, we would ask the creative people at Saquish to make an item of their specialty and donate it for the raffle. Then many people would win one or more of the items that were in the raffle. Chances would cost $1 apiece or 6 for $5. Again the residents responded with enthusiasm, both creatively and financially.

When we vacationed in Aruba, we collected many unique seashells. Ann made a shell mirror which was placed in the main bathroom of our cottage. Many of our friends commented on how beautiful that mirror looked. Ann decided to make a mirror for the first raffle. Over time, Ann's mirror and Fay Perry's handmade quilt became the prime items. They both turned into separate individual raffles. When you bought tickets you could use them for the general raffle, the mirror or the quilt. The raffle, with no expenses associated with it, had turned into a lucrative revenue stream.

It also created a small business for us. A number of people asked Ann to make and sell them a mirror. We owned two weeks of time-sharing in St. Maarten and when we went there, we would bring a suitcase full of items that we could not buy in St. Maarten. The first two years there we visited every beach on the island and found the ones with the best shelling. During the two weeks we would make frequent excursions to these beaches.

Many years we would also take a catamaran across a large open bay, visit St. Bart's and spend the whole day at Shell Beach collecting shells. This is one of the better shelling beaches in the world. Between both places we would find enough shells to fill the empty suitcase that brought the items that we used while we were there. One time an airport attendant thought I hit the "Jack Pot," and was bringing all the quarters back in the suitcase. That was before the airlines had any charge for overweight luggage or any charge for luggage at all.

On our trips to Florida, we would collect shells at Sanibel, Captiva and Cayo Costa Islands. Sanibel is considered the third best shelling place in the world. Scallop shells, which were used to outline both the extremities of the plywood backing and the mirror, were obtained from commercial scallopers in Welfleet, MA. and Nantucket Island. Moon shells, mussels and sand dollars came from Saquish. Small white shells that she collected at the Saquish Beach curve became her signature shell. We didn't know what its official name was, so Ann called it her "Special Saquish Shell." They were signed and placed near the bottom of her mirrors.

With these sources of shell supplies, the business grew. Besides people from Saquish and their friends, she received orders from a number of people who had seen her mirrors and wanted one packed and shipped to them. To handle this we had some shipping cartons made that would protect the shells and glass mirror during shipping.

There was a specialty shop on Cape Cod that took her mirrors on a consignment basis. In their shop they sold a glazed shell toilet seat and we swapped a mirror for one. It was placed in our main bathroom and often received as many comments as the mirrors. Ann also created a shell tree with fifty lights embedded in it. This is often given as a gift to our good friends on special occasions.

Each Spring, in Florida, there is a Sanibel Island Shell Fair. Competition is divided into two classes, amateur and professional. The fair attracts some of the best professional shell artists that do creative shell work for a living. Shell collectors also exhibit there. They come from as far away as Australia and China. On our most recent visit to the fair, we brought one of Ann's signature shells with us. We tried to find out what the shell's common name was and showed it to a number of shell experts. None of them could identify its common name, but a couple identified its scientific name and said it came from the northern Atlantic waters that were rocky. Scientifically, it was a member of the Norcella family of shells. With this initial piece of information, we looked on the internet, and found out that it has three common names. They are the dog whelk, the Atlantic dog winkle and the rock shell. Now we know the official name of the shell, but to Ann it will always be her "Special Saquish

Shell," found near The Gurnet rocks at the curve in the beach.

Ann had entered the fair for two years in a row. Since she had sold her work, she had to enter the professional division. The first year she entered a shell mirror, and received an Honorable Mention Ribbon. The judges said her work was very good, but that year they were focusing on and giving many points for creative design. That was the area in which she did not score well. The next year she entered her lighted shell tree and won a Second Place Red Ribbon. Not a bad record when going up against full-time professionals. Ann donated a shell mirror to the Saquish raffle for twenty-five years. It goes to show where a one time donation of a special creation can lead you.

Another fundraising endeavor was started by Ann and Paula Cavanaugh, one of her co-fund raising members. At that time, bake auctions were very popular to support charities or one time special events. So they decided to have the first Saquish Bake Auction. It was well advertised and a number of Saquish residents baked or prepared their specialty items. On a Saturday morning in August with Al Greymont as the auctioneer, over $1,100 was raised, again with no expense.

Many husbands bid up their wife's items to a high dollar amount. The bake sale was continued every other year since its inception. Homemade pies, especially Donna Brouillard's, often go for more than $100 apiece. During our last year at Saquish, Ann made an additional mirror which was donated for the bake auction. Jeannie Cotti-Johnson was the highest bidder. She and her husband Gary now display the mirror in their Florida home. As time went on, additional fund raising activities were started by other people and fund raising continues to make a major contribution to the revenue stream of The Gurnet Saquish Association.

Ann and I remained on the Board of Directors until we moved to Florida in the mid-nineties and then mainly summered at Saquish. Ann continued to work on fundraising activities and I stayed on the nominating committee for a few more years. More recently, I was a member of the Documents Revision Committee. To maintain our tax-free status, it was necessary to revise the documents and keep them consistent with the current state statutes. This was finally accomplished with Heather and Jerry Esposito heading up the activity. They spent a substantial amount of work and hours on the project, and deserve the major credit for its success.

Ann and I spent forty years at Saquish. We always believed that if you received something, you should give something back. The time and effort we spent working with The Gurnet-Saquish Association was our way of giving thanks for the wonderful life that Saquish and its residents provided for us.

CHAPTER 18
REMEMBRANCES

During the forty years we spent at Saquish, there were a number of experiences that although memorable, did not logically fit into any of the preceding chapters. This chapter covers those events.

LIGHTS OUT

One June evening in the early '70's, we had just moved to Saquish for the Summer. It was a pitch-dark night and we did not see lights in any of the cottages. All of a sudden we heard footsteps coming up the front stairs and onto our porch. They were followed by a loud knock on the door. We opened the door and there were two young woman we did not know. They were Jeannie Cotti and her sister. Their folks owned a cottage a little way from ours and the two of them came to spend a couple of days at the beach. Everything was going well for them until the gaslights dimmed and then went out. They were left in the dark.

They had no idea what to do. With a large flashlight they left their cottage and went looking for someone to help. Ours was the only cottage with lights showing in the windows. They came into our cottage and asked me for help. With a large flashlight, and Kathi and Lorri with me, we followed them back to their cottage. The first items I checked were the gas stove and refrigerator. Neither worked. I then went outside and found two 100-pound gas tanks connected to each other. One was empty and was turned on, the other was full but was turned off. It was a simple matter of closing the empty one and opening the full one. After returning to the house, I lit the gaslights, stove and refrigerator. The girls were back in business.

One of Jeannie's fondest memories of that evening occurred while I was outside dealing with the gas tanks. She had a flashlight that was on, and she intensely watched my two young daughters as they sat on her couch not saying a word. It appeared they were statues just staring at each other. They were two well-behaved but frightened little girls, while their dad was outside helping two damsels in distress.

JARTS AT DOREY'S

On Friday nights many of us would play jarts on the roadway in front of Mel Dorey's cottage, which was diagonally behind ours.

Jarts was a game similar to horseshoes. Instead of poles there were two round plastic rings. You threw two jarts which looked like arrows but were much heavier and shorter with a hard steel point. If the jart landed in the ring you earned 3 points, if it didn't you drew a blank. The team that reached 21 points won the match. You played with partners just like in horse shoes. The stakes were $1 per person per game. If your team won, you kept playing. The team that hadn't played for the longest time had the right to challenge the winners when a match was over.

Mel had a floodlight, run by a generator that lit the area. Spectators would sit on the sand dune on side of the sandy cart path. Quite often the game would continue well past midnight. Every now and then the players would get a little rowdy. This had nothing to do with drinking a few beers. The following day one of our neighbors would ask us to keep the noise down the next time we played. We tried. How successful we were is debatable!

THE BEACH PATROL

In the early years Mr. Stewart, an elderly gentleman and landowner visited Saquish at 10 o'clock every Sunday morning. He had an old Jeep and would ride from one end of the beach to the other traveling at 5 MPH. On a very low tide, he would drive all the way to Western Point. After going as far as the tide would permit, he would turn around and retrace his tracks, never changing his speed. This was before the 5 MPH speed limit for the plovers.

After Mr. Stewart stopped coming to Saquish, Billy Hartwick took up the activity of Beach Patrol. Billy, however, drove a little faster than Mr. Stewart, did it more often and at no defined times. He would often make two or three complete trips without stopping.

Both Mr. Stewart and Billy were fixtures and very much a part of Saquish history.

NEWSPAPERS AND DONUTS

During the mid-nineties Tammie Pink and her four children Bobby, Rachel, Cindy and Jason started a newspaper and donut business. Early Sunday morning they would drive to Duxbury, buy a number of Boston Globe newspapers and dozens of Dunkin Donuts. After returning to the beach, they would park in front of our cottage and sell the newspapers and donuts from the back of their SUV. This was quite a hit with people on the beach. The alternative was a round trip to town to buy a Sunday newspaper and donuts, which would take well over an hour.

When she sold out, a decent profit was made. When the weather was bad or for any other reason a surplus was left over, the profits diminished. Being an astute entrepreneur, Tammie decided to take orders and pre-charge for what you wanted the following weekend. Therefore you either picked them up or forfeited your payment. Tammie's profit was guaranteed and the children often had a late breakfast of fresh donuts, but they were not old enough to effectively read the newspaper. This went on for a number of years.

It was a sad Sunday morning when Tammie closed down the business.

THE SLEEPING BAG

One evening Ann had a sleepless night and decided to go into the kitchen and read. Our SUV was parked in back of the cottage. This was shortly after we had stopped parking it in the front. There was a full moon and Ann went to the front window to look at it and the reflection in the calm ocean.

Not only was the view spectacular, but she also noticed something in front of the cottage, where our car previously was parked. There was a sleeping bag with a person's head exposed. Some clothes were lying beside it. Ann called me and then went on the porch and yelled, "What are you doing here?" With that a second head popped up and said, "Please give us a chance to put our clothes on and we'll leave." We went back to bed and started to laugh. Another one of the humorous events that occurred at Saquish Beach.

Sorry about interrupting a good night's sleep!

PRAY FOR THE HOOKED DOG

Mike and Emma Simone along with Mike and Doris Grasseschi and their six children spent a weekend with us. Most of Saturday was spent cod fishing. After returning, the cod rigs were draped over the railing to dry out. Each rig had two large hooks on it.

That afternoon Tammie Pink's dog was running around on our porch. It brushed up against the railing and a hook from the rig caught the dog near the stomach. The dog tried to pull away from the rail and the more it pulled the deeper the hook penetrated, until the barb became lodged underneath the skin. We grabbed the dog and pinned it to the porch floor. He was whining and sweating profusely. The men held him to prevent any movement while Tammie tried to comfort him.

I went into the cottage, returned with some tools and then performed a simple medical procedure. The hook was pushed back up through the skin and cut off below the barb with large wire cutters. It was then easily extracted, the wound was smothered with peroxide and the dog was released.

By that time it was too late to drive off the beach and go to Mass. I offered to conduct a prayer service on the back porch and everyone agreed.

The service lasted about fifteen minutes and included a brief sermon. We all prayed that the dog would be O.K. and heal without any problems.

Our prayers were answered.

THE CANDY STORE

There is a cottage on Saquish Head called the Candy Store. While living at or visiting Saquish, children loved to go to the Candy Store and buy many different types of candy. A sign in front of the store identified whether the store was opened or closed, since the hours of operation were very flexible.

When children were returning from their trip to the store, a smile on their faces indicated the store was open, while a frown indicated it was closed.

THE TRIP THOUGH HELL

The first time the Halls and Gallos visited us, Dave Hall caught a 34-pound striper. Shortly thereafter he bought a boat, over twenty feet long. The next time they came to visit us Dave brought his boat. He planned to launch it from Duxbury and moor it in front of our cottage for the weekend. Early on Saturday morning, they arrived at the Duxbury Marina. The tide was so low that they couldn't launch the boat and wouldn't be able to for a few hours. Dave contacted me and I came out with my SUV to bring them to the beach.

We planned to take my boat and go back to Duxbury in the early afternoon and return with Dave's boat, hopefully doing some striper fishing on the way over or back. Later that morning a storm hit us with high winds and heavy rains. By mid-afternoon the rains had decreased and since the wind was coming from the North, there were no swells in front of our cottage.

Frank, Dave and I hopped into my boat and headed for Duxbury. We no sooner rounded the tip of Western Point and were headed due North when we ran directly into three foot-plus breaking swells, many of which sprayed and drenched us with water. The swells, the spraying and the drenching increased as we traversed the four miles across Duxbury Bay. At times we were concerned about not making it safely to the marina. Years of experience, calm nerves and a slow steady speed while bucking the waves at a 45 degree angle all helped. A couple of times we had to pull the drain plug to let water that had splashed over the sideboards, drain from the boat.

After arriving at Duxbury, we launched Dave's boat and attached my small boat to the back of his boat with a long rope. The ride back was with the wind and the swells. In the large boat we felt much safer, but a couple of times my small boat almost tipped over as it was being towed with no one steering it.

Once we made it back, Dave's boat sat on the mooring for the rest of the weekend. The weather never allowed us to go fishing or even lobstering.

When he took his crew back the next day the weather had somewhat subsided but it was not a pleasant ride and still very windy. Landing it at the dock and then getting the boat on the trailer proved to be quite a chore, since the wind continued to blow it sideways. Dave and his family had many enjoyable days on the boat. However, like many boat owners his two happiest days were the day he bought it and the day he sold it.

For some unknown reason Dave never again brought the boat to Saquish when he and his family came to visit us.

FORGETFUL

Marilyn and Ed McTighe visited us a number of times. Before they owned a 4-wheel drive they parked their car at the Duxbury High School parking lot. I would drive out to meet them and then after the visit take them back.

One time they ate as many lobsters as they could and there were still two left over. Ann wrapped them in aluminum foil and placed them in a plastic bag, right next to Marilyn who sat in the back seat. It would make good lobster salad for the McTighes after they returned home. We then drove them to Duxbury and returned to the beach.

After our SUV had sat in the sun for two days, Ann opened one of its doors. You have no idea what two lobsters wrapped in aluminum foil and exposed to the sunny conditions of a beach smelled like. On the bumpy road out the lobsters had slipped off the back seat and slid under the front seat. The same thing happened to Marilyn's small purse which contained her driver's license and she never realized it.

After backing a few feet away from the SUV and taking a few deep breaths of fresh ocean air, Ann called Marilyn. She was driving alone in her car and answered her cell phone. When Ann asked if she had forgotten anything when she was at Saquish a few days earlier, Marilyn said not that she could remember. When Ann told her what she had found, Marilyn was shocked. She apologized for the smell, was excited to get her license and purse back, but would have nothing to do with taking back the lobsters.

The SUV was cleaned and after leaving it in the fresh air for two days with the windows open, the smell returned to normal. The lobsters ended up as bait for the lobster pots, the next time I baited them. Everything recycles!

A LIFE SAVING EXPERIENCE

One day Gene Wojnar and I had just returned from cod fishing. Our fishing trip was cut short due to high winds and breaking waves that turned a mild ocean into a treacherous one.

We had just started to eat lunch when Alice Plimpton came running down the beach yelling that a boat had capsized in the bay. I ran out onto the porch and asked her where the boat was. She pointed out to the ocean where, from my high porch, I could see two elevated heads bobbing in the swells.

I took a reading, lining up the two heads with the corner of the porch and the mast of a catamaran that was resting on the beach and yelled to both Ethan and Ricky Balakier to get their boat in the water and join us. Gene and I were able to re-launch his boat through the breaking waves and following my reading headed into the bay. The swells were rough, but I finally saw two men trying to hang onto a lobster buoy.

All of a sudden the older man slipped under the water and the younger one, who appeared to be the strongest, was able to reach down into the water and pull the head back up, while still holding on to the lobster buoy with his other hand. This happened again. They were facing away from us toward the main channel where a large boat was just returning to Plymouth Harbor. The younger man would try to wave at the large boat as he continued to hold on to the older one. This was a Herculean effort just to keep the older man from sinking under the water and being sucked away with the swift current and breaking swells. The returning boat never saw them as it continued on its straight line path toward Plymouth Harbor.

With the wind blowing against us, they couldn't hear me yelling until we were fifteen feet away from them. Once they heard me, the younger man who was still hanging onto the older man quickly turned to face us. The expression on his face turned from despair to an expression of hope. I threw him a life preserver cushion. Gene helped the younger man into the boat, while I grabbed the older man by the hair. Due to the size of the man and the breaking waves, this was the best way to hold his head above water until Ethan and Ricky pulled alongside.

They were able to roll the older man over the edge and into their boat, almost tipping it over. We took the two survivors back to shore, where they received assistance, including warm blankets, from the residents.

All's well that ends well.

BEACH PLUM JELLY

Beach Plums are a fruit that grows wild on the peninsula. Their bushes are often entangled with thick poison ivy vines. Many people pick them and make Beach Plum Jelly, our granddaughter Sydney's favorite jelly! Shirley Rushton and Peggy Sayce made excellent Beach Plum Jelly. It's great when spread on toast and eaten for breakfast.

Before leaving for Florida, Ann and I would try to acquire enough to last the Winter. Unfortunately, many times we'd run out before we returned to Saquish in the Spring.

THE MAYOR OF SAQUISH

Many communities have someone who has spent a number of years living there, knows its history, and goes out of their way to enhance its image and protect its environment. This person is respectively known as "The Mayor." They are not necessarily a politician, but the name and reputation are remembered for a long time.

Warren Rushton is often referred to as the "Mayor of Saquish." Shirley Rushton's parents owned a cottage at Saquish before she was born and she grew up there. When she married Warren, he quickly adopted Saquish and its environment as a major part of his life. Shirley has spent her lifetime there and Warren has been there for sixty years.

When anyone or a group of people were littering the beach or damaging the sand dunes, Warren had a unique way of convincing them that what they were doing was wrong. More often than not, they would pick up the mess they had created and leave the beach. Some of his stories regarding these occurrences are both interesting and humorous.

Warren's door was always open and when you stopped by, you were immediately offered a drink. He enjoyed social visits as well as visits to discuss beach situations. If you asked a question, you always received an answer. It would either be direct or philosophical. In either case you would get an answer to your question.

On New Year's Day Warren and Shirley have an open house at their cottage and everyone who comes to the beach stops by for a visit. They are fine representatives of the Saquish tradition.

"Warren, this drink is a toast to you!"

MARGARITAVILL

Shortly after building our cottage we discovered that Margarita Parties were common at Saquish. They were often hosted by Mike and Estella Jenness along with John and Charlotte Devir. Both couples were fixtures on the beach, and they made superb Margaritas. The parties were well attended and enjoyable. There was one party however that specifically stands out in my memory.

John hosted a Margarita Party for his wife Charlotte on one of her special birthdays. Charlotte loved the color purple. To attend the party you had to wear a type of clothing that was purple. People showed up with shoes, hats, shorts, jerseys, barrettes and other pieces of clothing that were purple in color. Some were dyed and others were in their natural state. Gifts were the same, all purple. It looked like a wave of purple had washed up from the sea onto John's cottage porch.

John's Margaritas were again superb. As the afternoon wore on, some of us thought that John might have some

Biblical powers. As good as the first Margarita was, each additional one tasted better than the previous one.

As the party neared the end, many of us wondered whether we were still at John's cottage or whether we were "WASTING AWAY AGAIN IN MARGARITAVILLE."

THE NOVELIST

As a boy, Peter Endicott had many cousins and friends that had cottages at Saquish, and he spent a number of Summers there. After he married Sherry and had four sons, he and his family rented a cottage on Saquish for three Summers. The cottage was right next to ours. Each Summer we enjoyed talking with Peter, Sherry and their four sons while they were vacationing. Peter and his family then bought a cottage and made Saquish a major part of their family life.

Peter has recently written a novel titled RIPPLES, it's a very enjoyable book. The main characters are a twelve-year old boy and his friends. The setting is Gurnet Point, Saquish Beach, Clark's Island and the surrounding waters. The plot is to unravel some mysteries they have dredged up from the muddy depths of the sea.

When Peter heard I was writing this book, he stopped by a couple of times to see me. His knowledge and experience proved very helpful. He reminded me about the time we were on our porches talking about fishing. He had caught many flounder and cod but had never caught a striped bass. I offered to take him fishing if he would meet me the next morning one hour before sunrise. He went on to say that I had guaranteed him that he would then catch his first striped bass. The next morning we started out one hour before sunrise. On the second or third drift through the rip-tide at Western Point, Peter caught a 26" striped bass, his first but not his last.

Peter is thinking about writing a sequel. I hope he does and look forward to reading it!

STITCHES AND BROKEN BONES

During our 40 years at Saquish, Jordan Hospital was a place we visited quite often. Not that we enjoyed it, but the Emergency Room provided excellent care.

Our visits started during our very first Summer when Lorri sliced her finger on a razor clam. During the forty years, I accumulated a number of major cuts, bruises and infections working around the cottage, lobstering and cleaning fish. Jordan Hospital went with the territory. The most common requirement for stitches was hitting my head on a sharp floor joist while working under the cottage. The trip to the hospital took over half a day. Ann never learned how to put in stitches, but became very adept at removing them. This eliminated one of the two half-day trips.

Ann never had an accident that required stitches. However broken bones were a different matter. A few years ago we started to close the cottage and pack for Florida. We had planned to stop in Connecticut and attend Ann's 45th Year High School Reunion.

I was upstairs in the observation room watching a Patriot's game. Ann was downstairs and stood on a chair to put a pie plate on the upper shelf of a kitchen cabinet. All of a sudden there was a loud crash and yell! She had somehow slipped off the chair and was sprawled out on the kitchen floor. Luckily her head had missed the counter top when she fell. She lay there twisting and turning in excruciating pain.

Sandy Keegan and I assisted and tried to comfort her. We then helped her hobble on one foot to the back porch, down the steps and into the SUV. The pain intensified with the bumpy trip over The Gurnet Road. Sandy had called an ambulance and it met us in the Duxbury Beach parking lot. The EMT's checked her out and then took off for Jordan Hospital. I couldn't keep up with them and I'm not a slow driver.

There were two broken bones in her left leg. She was placed in a cast and given a pair of crutches. We then returned to Saquish. Our trip to Florida was delayed and there was no going to the high school reunion. The next two weeks were spent at appointments with an orthopedic surgeon. During that time Lorri flew over from Nantucket and helped pack our clothing, supplies and other items for our return trip to Florida. Sandy Keegan and Sandy Wojnar were a great help in closing down the cottage. Anna Hartwick, who had much experience in packing an SUV came to help. Ann sat in a chair on the back porch and directed the packing effort. I carried the items down the back steps. With much finesse, Anna squeezed everything into the SUV. There wasn't any room to spare, but enough was left for Ann to lean back in the seat and stretch out her legs.

The orthopedic surgeon would not let Ann fly to Florida. She could, however, ride in the SUV as long as we stopped every two hours and let her stretch out and relax for one half hour. We stopped at many highway rest areas and used the picnic benches to do this. The trip took more than twice as long as usual.

The last night we stayed at a motel in Jacksonville, Florida. The next morning we ate breakfast at the motel's restaurant and Ann used her crutches to reach the restroom. They had just cleaned their bathroom floor with a liquid that was very slippery. When Ann went into a stall and locked the door, her crutches slipped out and she fell face first to the floor. She laid there yelling until someone in the adjoining men's room heard her and called the motel personnel. I then saw a commotion in front of the restroom as the personnel were helping Ann.

She felt O.K. so we continued our drive to Fort Myers. Once there we went to the Emergency Room at Health Park for a checkup. The x-rays were negative. Just as he was about to release Ann, the attending doctor changed his mind. Due to everything she had told him, he wanted to be absolutely sure that no blood clot had formed. One last test was taken an ultra-sound, which turned out to be positive.

After five days in the hospital and three months of physical therapy Ann was back to her healthy, active self. During the recuperation period in Florida the response of our friends at Kelly Greens was awesome. Many friends brought tasty meals, and helped by running errands, which were greatly appreciated.

This is typical of the supportive people and nature of our community.

FRIENDS FROM KELLY GREENS

In 1989 after touring Florida, Ann and I bought a condo at Kelly Greens Golf and Country Club. It is located in southwest Fort Myers near the Sanibel, Captiva and Fort Myers Beaches. The golf course and restaurant are top notch and the recreational activities that are provided meet a host of needs. After I retired in 1992, this became our winter home.

From that time on, a number of our Kelly Greens friends have spent time with us at Saquish. They all enjoyed the beach activities. They included fishing, clamming, lobstering, walking the beach, picnicking at Gurnet Light, visiting downtown Plymouth, seeing Plymouth Rock and the replica of the Mayflower. Eating at Izacck's Restaurant was also a treat.

One of the most enjoyable activities of all was just plain socializing. The most interesting was lobstering since no one had previously experienced it. For each couple or group that visited, there were one or more unique experiences or activities that are worth mentioning.

Don and Jane Hanks were two of our first friends at Kelly Greens. Don could trace his family history back to Benjamin Hanks. According to the recorded deeds, sales and purchases of land at Saquish, Benjamin Hanks bought all the uplands on the peninsula in 1742. When Don and Jane were attending a Hank's family reunion in Plymouth, they had a chance to spend a few days with us at Saquish. On the way to Western Point there is a road named Hanks Avenue. It goes from Saquish Beach to the Back Bay. Don is one and might be the only one of Benjamin's recent descendants to see the beach property that Benjamin once owned.

We met Terry and Coco Gilbert the first Winter we stayed at Kelly Greens. The following Summer, after Coco attended a business meeting in Hartford, they came to visit us in Westboro. They helped us take some furniture, from our Westboro home which we were selling, to Bev McNair's home in Duxbury where it was stored until our observation room was built. From there all of us spent a couple of days enjoying the beach.

A number of years later they along with Coco's daughter Dani, Harris Turer and their two children Brandon and Gaby attended a Red Sox game in Boston. Harris and Brandon were making visits to as many major league baseball parks as possible. They were able to add Fenway Park to their list. After the game they all joined us at Saquish before moving on to add the name of another ballpark to the list that they were compiling.

Ann and I along with Della and Vance Fisher, Terry and Bob Patrick, and Ed and Cindy Fleisch played golf together once a month. One year we invited all of them to spend a few days with us at Saquish the following Summer. Before their leaving to visit us, something came up and the Patricks had to cancel.

I met the rest of them at the Duxbury Police Station where they were able to leave their car. Hearsay has it that the police had a hard time convincing Ed that there was no way he could drive his normal car to Saquish. I picked them up in my SUV and on the drive out Della bounced up and down every time we hit a bump. Evidently she had never ridden a horse and gained the experience of a bumpy ride.

When we arrived at Saquish, Della was the first one to enter the cottage and was given the choice of bedrooms to make up for the bumpy ride. Vance was fascinated by the sign that was on the wall in our main bathroom. With a shallow well and much company, water was a precious resource. The sign read, "When it's Yellow, Let it Mellow, When it's Brown, Flush it Down." Being from West Virginia, Vance really knew what that meant.

A couple of years later, Cindy and Ed bought a new all-wheel drive SUV. They all came back to visit us, this time including the Patrick's. Ed was convinced that his all-wheel drive could go anywhere a 4-wheel drive could. I cautioned Ed about this.

On the morning they were planning to arrive, I had to go into town to buy some supplies. If they arrived before my return, they were to park in front of the cottage and use the path that went up the sand dune and then to the cottage. They were not to drive around to the back of the cottage, as I had previously done with my 4-wheel drive when they were here on their first trip. After I returned from town we would check the all-wheel drive's capabilities to maneuver in the soft sand and then decide what it could do. When they arrived Ed pulled up in front of the cottage and Terry expressed some concern about climbing the soft sand dune. She asked if there was another way to access the cottage.

Ed did not exactly have the patience of Job. If Guinness had a listing for the man with the least patience, Ed would be in the running. After waiting a few minutes he turned the SUV around and rushed it up the side cart path that led to the back of the cottage. When he hit the 90 degree turn the sand was deep and soft. The SUV immediately bogged down. Ed then floored it and accelerated to maximum speed. The only problem was it only went twelve inches, straight down and then immediately stopped and was buried up to the frame. When I returned from town, my Florida friends were with a number of my Saquish neighbors digging out Ed's SUV. For the rest of the time the SUV was parked in front of the cottage.

Everywhere Ed went, he always left or did something for the locals to remember him. At Saquish the 90 degree turn at the intersection of the soft, sandy cart paths became known as "Ed's Corner." At Saquish Ed was remembered for years.

Della was the first one into the cottage and again had the choice of bedrooms. Vance checked to be sure his favorite sign was still in the bathroom. Bob, as usual, took a host of excellent pictures, and gave copies to all. Terry learned how to climb up and down the soft sand dune. On a picnic to Gurnet Light, Cindy had the experience of riding in the cargo area of my pickup truck. Sitting on a plastic bucket, while going over bumpy roads and riding in a truck with bad shock absorbers was quite an experience. This made it more like riding a bucking bronco rather than a horse. By the time we returned, Cindy was sore from head to toe, including her backside. We had many laughs and enjoyed the whole endeavor.

One summer our Canadian friends, Larry and Eva Godfree joined us. Larry had not slept well for a long time, but on the first night while sleeping in the cottage, surrounded by the clean ocean air, he had a very restful sleep. The next morning it was clear and bright with a calm ocean, so we all hopped into my boat and headed across the bay to see Historic Plymouth and have lunch at Izacck's restaurant. We docked at the Plymouth Town Mooring. After returning that afternoon Larry took a nap on a lounge chair that was on the front porch. With the warm clean ocean breeze he had one of the best naps ever, it was even better than the sleep he had the night before. That night he didn't sleep inside the cottage, but instead slept outside on the lounge chair. It was the best night's sleep he ever had. For the rest of the time, whenever there was a break in activities, Larry filled it with an outside nap. By the time they left Larry and Eva were well rested. Just like many of our guests, the Godfrees had found the clean beach air and warm breezes perfect for sleeping.

Curt and Judy Repass flew from Chicago to visit. I had just bought blinds for the back windows of our observation room. Curt's help and expertise saved me many hours of frustration in installing them. After a couple of days, Judy made the comment. "The ride in and staying on the beach was a religious experience." This paralleled something Ann had said for years, which is "Saquish is the closest place to Heaven on Earth." Although they both expressed it differently, they are both right.

When John and Gail McCluer came to Saquish, John took a picture of Gail that he treasures. The picture is framed and on display in their den. Gail is sitting in front of my boat holding up a large lobster. We had just gone lobstering and were returning with dinner. She is wearing a big hat to protect her from the sun and looks very hungry. Sorry Gail, it is still three hours till dinner. To make up for the delay, I'll prepare two lobsters that you can eat for dinner this evening.

Ray and Judy Kwiatkowski spent a few days with us. Ray was more fascinated with lobstering and lobsters than anyone else. They might have reminded him of some middle line backers he had coached. They crouched low to the ground, had big powerful claws that were quick but they lacked lateral speed.

You could tell he had never spent time on a remote beach. One morning he wondered down to the beach shortly after the tide had started to recede, stood between two freshly made tire tracks and made a cell phone call to his brother. A resident who was driving the second vehicle to use the same path had to pull out to get by Ray. After pulling out, the driver stopped beside Ray, rolled down the window, gave Ray a dirty look and yelled, "Get out of the road." Ray stood there in a state of shock but fortunately he did not utter a word or lose his temper. Ray never realized that the tide had just receded and he was now standing in the middle of the Boulevard, the main highway across Saquish Beach. Anyone who had spent time on a remote beach would have known that after seeing the new tire tracks.

Except for the person that yelled at Ray, both he and Judy enjoyed the calm quiet serenity of the beach and its environment.

Cindy Fleisch returned for the third time. She came with Ken and Sue Greves along with Jeanne Shilling. We spent much time sitting in the observation room admiring the view and socializing. We also toured the historic sites of downtown Plymouth. The New England Clam Chowder at Izacck's Restaurant was the best they ever had. One morning Ken went out on the beach and took many pictures of our cottage. After returning to Florida he had Jimmy Serdenis, a Kelly Greens resident and professional artist, do a pen and ink drawing of the cottage. It is now displayed in our Florida Sun Room.

SALES MEETINGS AT SAQUISH

I was part of a large sales and technical support organization that lived or died by meeting or not meeting its sales objective. My objective was the cumulative sum of all the individual objectives in the organization. With much hard work and a little luck we always met our goals.

For a number of years, in the Summer, I would have a sales meeting with my management team at Saquish. The business meeting was short and the rest of the day was spent enjoying ourselves.

One year my Staff Manager, Harry Vafides, suggested that we have the whole organization join us at the meeting. I said that was not possible. The problem was that we would need more than ten 4-wheel drives, and the workload to cook the meals was more than Ann and I could handle. It was just not feasible.

At the managers meeting the following week, Harry stated that my problems were solved. I didn't know I had problems, not even one problem. My staff however always tried to address a situation and put it to bed before it became a problem. So I listened!

He and my Secretary Mamie Lawn had canvased the whole organization, located enough 4-wheel drives and volunteers to do the cooking. They would also take care of all the necessary arrangements. This seemed interesting so I discussed the possibility with Ann. She thought it was great to meet and spend some social time with many of the people in the organization. With that concurrence, I agreed with one provision. It was that the sales organization must have one half of its annual sales objective met by the end of June. If not, the meeting would not take place and instead we would have a normal work day. The meeting date was set for the first Thursday in August, just prior to my two week Summer vacation. This agreement with my management team existed until I retired.

One year we were not on target at the end of June. Before I cancelled the summer sales meeting, the managers made me an offer. If we had the Saquish Sales Meeting they assured me that we would meet the year-end objective. They backed this up by putting their jobs on the line. We all knew from our quarterly sales reviews what was in the pipeline, so I accepted their offer. What arrangements the managers had with their account executives were up to them, however in the second half of the year everyone worked as hard as I had ever seen. Needless to say, at the end of the year no one lost their job.

Attendance at the meeting was optional and a few people had to stay back and cover the office. After starting with coffee, juice, donuts, bagels and muffins, the business meeting began. I would talk from the porch and the attendees would sit on the sand dune in front and listen. The business meeting and speech was short. Ann would then join me and we would thank them for working hard to make their and our sales objective. This day was Ann and my time to give something back to the people who worked with me. Their success was my success. The short meeting was followed by activities of their choice. They included clamming, swimming, taking a walk along the beach, card playing, volleyball, horseshoes and laying in the sun or shade and just plain relaxing.

At midday a committee prepared hot dogs, hamburgers and salads for lunch on our grill and a couple of grills we borrowed from neighbors. Dinner consisted of a choice of lobsters, steaks or chicken. There were many more requests for lobster than I could catch and store in my keeper pot. To account for this, I made arrangements with a local fish market to pick up as many lobsters as was needed the afternoon before the meeting. They were then taken to Saquish and stored overnight in the keeper pot to keep them fresh until the next day. As the reputation of this annual meeting grew a number of people, who supported our organization but were in other divisions of the company, lobbied for an invitation to attend the summer sales meeting. The criteria used to attend was very rigid and was based on providing a substantial amount of support. One year there were 73 people that stayed for dinner, with just a few that were not part of the organization.

It was amazing what people learned about each other. In this one-day of social interaction they found out what their co-workers were like, outside of a work environment. This carried forth to the work environment and often made it easier to accomplish things. Many friendships were developed. These were the generic thoughts I heard most often from the people. The Saquish Sales Meetings were not only the highlight of the year for the sales organization, but for me they were at the top of the most enjoyable days in my whole business career.

Thank you Harry, Mamie and all of you that attended the meetings. You helped to make this such a memorable event.

CLASS OF 1961 SKULLS REUNIONS

During my Senior year at WPI, I, along with nine others, were members of a special organization known as THE SKULL. Through the many Skull activities we became a very close group.

After graduating, a number of us and our spouses returned every fifth year for a reunion. At the 30th year reunion, it was suggested that we meet more often than once every five years, so Ann and I offered to host a reunion the following Summer at our remote cottage on Saquish Beach

Over half the group and their spouses attended and spent the weekend at the cottage. Dick and Sheila Adler, due to a scheduling conflict, could not come for the weekend but drove up from New York on Sunday to attend that day's activities. We clammed, fished, lobstered, walked the beach, picnicked and socialized. We even had time for a beer or two. Just a wonderful time. From then on, we decided to hold a get together every year, if possible. So it happened.

Some of the highlights of the next twenty years were the time we spent at Paul and Gaby Sledzik's condo in Los Palmas Del Mar, Puerto Rico. A week of fun in the sea and the sun. The golfing was not bad either.

Then there were the days and nights at Joe and Joan Carpentiere's Bed and Breakfast in Beaufort, South Carolina. What a casual relaxing atmosphere and a memorable time.

Another reunion was at Mo and Jan Rees' home in Alexandria, Virginia. It provided a chance to experience American history at its best. Unfortunately, Ann and I could not attend that year.

Brad and Nita Hosmer along with George and Dottie Foxhall hosted us in New Hampshire with much time spent at George and Dottie's summer home on Mirror Lake. There's nothing like riding in a motorboat on a calm fresh water lake on a bright sunny afternoon.

Mel and Mary Kay Keegan lived in California, and we planned to hold our 2001 reunion there. Their daughter and our daughter lived in San Francisco and that was where we planned to have the reunion. Hotel arrangements were made there for those planning to attend. The date was set for mid-September. Unfortunately the event of 9/11 forced most of our group to cancel their plans. Ann and I flew to San Francisco and the Keegans flew in from Los Angeles. Only four people, but still a reunion and a chance to relive some old times along with bringing each other up to date.

For the last number of years Mo and Jan Rees have rented a cottage on Cape Cod every Fall. That was the focus of our more recent reunions, with Jan really holding the group together. They were supported by Bill and Betty Calder, Jack and Marilyn Gabarro along with Paul and Gaby Sledzik. They all had homes on the Cape.

On Friday of our 2009, reunion we spent the day at Saquish, where it all started, before going to the Cape. Ann asked us to move a very heavy old wooden bucket filled with loam and flowers. The moving distance was about 20 feet. She suggested that we use two by fours, placed underneath, to support it.

Six engineers, with close to 300 years of experience knew better. We decided to just reach underneath the bucket, pick it up and carry it. Halfway there the bucket just collapsed. Shows what 300 years of engineering experience is worth.

However, the excuse was that a large majority of those years were spent in non-engineering disciplines. From there we moved on to Cape Cod.

Lately the main event at the reunions has turned into pure socialization. There is often a round of golf at Paul's private golf course on the Cape. Every now and then we go to dinner at a quaint restaurant. There were many, good interesting times but one that is worth mentioning.

One Saturday afternoon, at Jack's home in Chatham, we were invited to play croquet. Most of us had not played croquet for a long time. It appeared it was that long since Jack had mowed his lawn. He had a hand mower in his shed, which was broken. With the wealth of engineering talent available it was fixed in nothing flat. Quite a difference from the screw up when carrying the wooden bucket. We then made lanes between the wickets, jolting the lawn mower two or three feet at a time. There were many laughs that afternoon.

The croquet match was a success. If croquet ever becomes an Olympic sport, the Skull has a team that's ready for the trials.

Today is September 22 the autumnal Equinox. Summer is changing to Fall. In just two days, Ann and I will drive from Florida, North to Massachusetts.

We'll go to Nantucket to see Lorri, Brian and our two grandchildren. We'll spend time with Miss Sydney, my favorite granddaughter, and see Cory play in three Junior High football games. From there it's back to Saquish to enjoy a few days with friends. After that, it's on to Cape Cod to join Jan, Mo and five other couples for another Skull reunion.

Finally we'll attend the Fifty Year Anniversary of Sandy and Gene Wojnar's wedding-the event at which Ann and I first met fifty years ago.

THE AUTHOR AND ANN

ABOUT THE AUTHOR

The author is married to Ann and they have two daughters Kathi and Lorri. He graduated from WPI with a degree in Electrical Engineering but spent his professional career in the Marketing and Sales disciplines.

During World War II his dad was conscripted by the government to work, under their control, as a private contractor. His last assignment was at Camp Edwards on Cape Cod. While there, his dad rented a cottage near the ocean. As a young boy, the author spent two Summers living there with his family. He fell in love with the ocean and dreamed of one day owning a cottage on an ocean beach.

While at WPI he was selected, along with nine others, to join an organization known as THE SKULL. During the initiation process he learned a significant lesson that stayed with him all his life. It was, "If you want to do something hard enough and you make a commitment to do it, you at times can accomplish what initially seemed impossible."

His wife Ann also loved the ocean, so when they had a chance to buy land and build a cottage at Saquish Beach, it was an opportunity they could not pass up. It would be a wonderful place for them to raise their two young daughters.

Saquish is located on a remote peninsula only thirty miles southeast of Boston. It has no town roads or services. Commercial electricity and land line telephone service were not available. You had to drive five miles using a 4-wheel drive vehicle to get there. During high tides it was often inaccessible.

The author writes about the times he and his family spent there during the forty years. He relives the memories, observations and experiences in building a cottage and participating in a host of activities on a remote beach.

He and Ann are now retired and live in Fort Myers, Florida.

Printed in the USA
CPSIA information can be obtained
at www.ICGtesting.com
LVHW011221150524
779807LV00001B/34